EASY HOME SEWING PROJECTS

Easy Home Sewing Projects

CompanionHouse Books™ is an imprint of Fox Chapel Publishers International Ltd.

Project Team
Vice President–Content: Christopher Reggio
Editor: Amy Deputato
Copy Editor: Kaitlyn Ocasio
Design: Mary Ann Kahn
Index: Elizabeth Walker

ISBN 978-1-62008-284-3

Library of Congress Cataloging-in-Publication Data

Names: Moorby, Charlie, author.
Title: Easy home sewing projects : 101 projects to transform every room of
   your home / by Charlie Moorby.
Description: Mount Joy, PA : Fox Chapel Publishers International Ltd., 2018.
   | Includes index.
Identifiers: LCCN 2017058054 (print) | LCCN 2017059587 (ebook) | ISBN
   9781620082850 (ebook) | ISBN 9781620082843 (softcover)
Subjects: LCSH: Sewing. | Needlework--Patterns. | House furnishings.
Classification: LCC TT715 (ebook) | LCC TT715 .M66 2018 (print) | DDC
   746.4--dc23
LC record available at https://lccn.loc.gov/2017058054

This book has been published with the intent to provide accurate and authoritative information in regard to the subject matter within. While every precaution has been taken in the preparation of this book, the author and publisher expressly disclaim any responsibility for any errors, omissions, or adverse effects arising from the use or application of the information contained herein.

Fox Chapel Publishing
903 Square Street
Mount Joy, PA 17552

Fox Chapel Publishers International Ltd.
7 Danefield Road, Selsey (Chichester)
West Sussex PO20 9DA, U.K.

www.facebook.com/companionhousebooks

We are always looking for talented authors. To submit an idea, please send a brief inquiry to acquisitions@foxchapelpublishing.com.

Printed and bound in Singapore
21 20 19 18   2 4 6 8 10 9 7 5 3 1

EASY HOME SEWING PROJECTS

101 Projects to Transform Every Room of Your Home

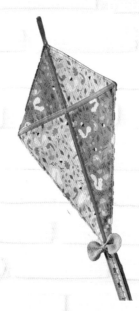

Charlie Moorby

CONTENTS

UPSTAIRS

BOLD BOUDOIR: BRIGHT BEDROOM DESIGNS • 8
Pillowcases ▪ Fabric Tassels ▪ Laundry Bag ▪ Lampshade
Pillowcase with Tassels ▪ Fabric-Mounted Picture Frame

FRESH LOOKS: PROJECTS FOR THE SECOND-FLOOR ROOMS • 24
Fabric Boxes ▪ Tissue-Box Cover ▪ Patchwork Towel
Toilet-Paper-Roll Holder ▪ Appliqué Towel ▪ Bolster Cushion
Bench Cushion ▪ Banner

COZY COVER-UP • 48
Hot-Water-Bottle Cover

PRETTY IN PINK: PASTEL SHADES FOR A RELAXING BEDROOM • 52
Bed Runner ▪ Cloud Cushions ▪ Beanbag ▪ Covered Notebooks
Storage Trays ▪ Coat Hangers

TIME TO PLAY: NURSERY TOYS AND DECORATIONS • 70
Geometric Bunting ▪ Kite Height Chart ▪ Play Mat
Jigsaw Cushions ▪ Stacking Rings ▪ Stool Covers

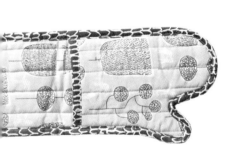

DOWNSTAIRS

KITCHEN BRIGHTS: UPDATE THE HEART OF YOUR HOME • 92
Pot Holders ▪ Oven Mitts ▪ Apron ▪ Plastic-Bag Holder
Tea Cozy ▪ Dish Towel

CREATIVE COASTERS: FUN WITH FELT WEAVING • 110
Coasters

THE PERFECT SETTING: CREATE BEAUTIFUL TABLE LINENS • 114
Zigzag Napkin ▪ Frayed Napkin ▪ Hemstitch Napkin
Basket Liner ▪ Place Mat ▪ Chair Cover ▪ Table Runner

DECOR FOR DOORS: SHOW YOUR DOORS SOME LOVE! • 132
Door Muffler ▪ Doorstop ▪ Draft Stopper

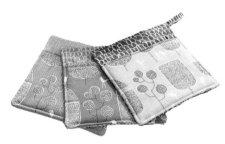

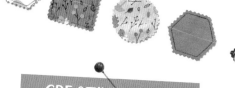

CREATIVE SPACES

FABRIC COVERS: GIVE YOUR SEWING ROOM A MAKEOVER • 144
Sewing-Machine Cover ▪ Fabric Letters ▪ Cord Organizer
Ironing-Board Organizer ▪ Ironing-Board Cover
Sewing Pinafore

PERFECT POCKETS: UPCYCLE YOUR JEANS • 162
Wall Organizer

WORK IT!: REVAMP YOUR HOME OFFICE • 168
Backpack ▪ Magazine File ▪ Binder Cover
Desk Organizer ▪ Slogan Banner ▪ Office Organizer

LOOK SHARP: A PRETTY PADDED SCISSOR CASE • 186
Scissor Case

GREAT OUTDOORS: A SET OF AL FRESCO ACCESSORIES • 190
Garden Cushion ▪ Windbreak ▪ Picnic Blanket
Duffel Bag ▪ Deck-Chair Sling

ESSENTIAL KNOW-HOW

THE GUIDE: STITCHES, TIPS, TECHNIQUES • 208

TEMPLATES • 216

INDEX • 222

ABOUT THE AUTHOR • 224

UPSTAIRS

From the bedroom to the bathroom via the nursery and landing, get set to show your second-floor rooms some fabulous fabric love!

BOLD BOUDOIR

BRIGHT BEDROOM DESIGNS

Add tassels, pictures, and hoops
for a boho bedroom makeover
in eye-catching colors!

Designer: Rebecca Reid **Styling:** Louise Day **Photography:** Philip Sowels

COLORFUL PILLOWCASES

We love the way these fabric inserts look like there's one pillowcase inside another! We've gone for bold brights as our main casing; for a more subtle look, use a bright accent as the insert and a softer shade for the main case.

TASSEL-TASTIC!

Tassels make a change from bunting and are a fun way of using up fabric scraps. If you want yours to coordinate with a room, simply buy extras of your favorite prints to cut into strips. And try yarn tassels on pillows!

LIGHT WORK

Coordinate your bedside table lamp with your bedding and accessories with this simple technique for covering most lampshade shapes. Add a ribbon edging in a contrasting color for a modern twist.

BRIGHT BEDROOM

HOOPS OF FUN

This ingenious laundry basket uses a large embroidery hoop. It keeps dirty laundry hidden away and even provides potential play as a basketball-style receptacle for shooting your socks into!

PRETTY AS A PICTURE...

If, like us, you've been meaning to make some fab fabric pictures for ages but haven't quite gotten around to it, now's the time! You can buy cheap picture frames that, with the right fabrics, will look good in any room. Our no-sew method really can be done in minutes.

PILLOWCASES

Turn your finished pillowcase right side out, with the lining fabric inside. When you put your pillow inside, make sure the lining fabric encases the end of the pillow.

YOU WILL NEED

- Standard pillowcase, 20 x 30 inches (50 x 75 cm)
- Contrast fabric (see instructions for sizing)
- Matching sewing thread

MEASUREMENTS

Standard pillowcase size, 20 x 30 inches (50 x 75 cm)

MAKING EACH PILLOWCASE

Step 1: Turn your pillowcase inside out and undo the side seams. One of the short edges will already be hemmed, and the other has a large pocket to slip your pillowcase in. Cut the pocket edge to meet up with the other edge, but cut it 1 inch (2½ cm) longer to allow for the hem. Turn over the edge by ½ inch (1¼ cm) and then by ½ inch (1¼ cm) again; from there, stitch down. The two ends of your pillowcase will now be the same length. (Fig. 1)

Step 2: Measure across the hemmed edge of your pillowcase and cut your lining fabric to this length and 18 inches (46 cm) wide. On your lining fabric, turn both long edges over ½ inch (1¼ cm) and then ½ inch (1¼ cm) again to the wrong side; press and then stitch these hems into place. (Fig. 2)

Step 3: Fold the lining fabric in half lengthwise with right sides together. With your pillowcase inside out, place it inside the folded lining fabric, making sure the two hemmed edges are all the way up inside the fold, aligning the side edges of the pillowcase and lining fabric. Stitch together down both side seams of the pillowcase, through all layers of pillowcase and lining fabric. (Fig. 3)

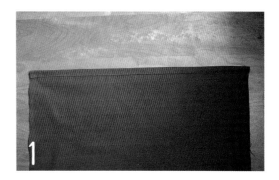

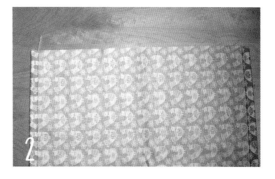

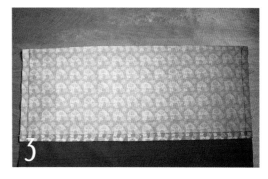

Choose lining fabric with a bold contrast pattern.

FABRIC TASSELS

The frayed fabric edges add a softer texture.

Make as many tassels as you want and then string them together through the loops at the top.

YOU WILL NEED

For one tassel

Cotton fabric,
14 x 20 inches (36 x 50 cm)

MEASUREMENTS

Each tassel measures 7 inches
(18 cm) long.

MAKING EACH TASSEL

Step 1: Fold your fabric in half lengthwise with wrong sides together. (Fig. 1)

Step 2: Cut into the fabric to form strips ¼ inch (2 cm) wide—start cutting at the open edge and stop 1½ (4 cm) from the fold. Cut the final strip off completely; you will use this to tie up your tassel. (Fig. 2)

Step 3: Open up your cut fabric and lay it flat, right side down, on your table. (Fig. 3)

Step 4: Starting at one end, roll up the fabric tightly, straightening out the strips as you go so they do not get tangled in each other. At the end, fold the raw fabric edge under and roll over it. (Fig. 4)

Step 5: Fold the rolled fabric in half with the end you turned under on the inside. (Fig. 5)

Step 6: Take the strip you cut off earlier and wrap it around the rolled-up fabric, approximately 1 inch (2½ cm) from the top. Wrap tightly to form the tassel. Fold under the short end and hold securely in place with a few small stitches. (Fig. 6)

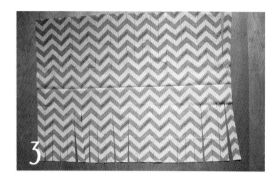

LAUNDRY BAG

The lining will be on display as much as the outer bag.

Tie a length of ribbon around the screw and hang it up to make a laundry bag that's always open.

YOU WILL NEED

- Gray cotton fabric, 2 pieces 27 x 19 inches (68 x 48 cm) for outer bag
- Orange cotton fabric, 2 pieces 27 x 19 inches (68 x 48 cm) for bag lining
- Wooden embroidery hoop, 10 inches (25 cm)
- Ribbon to hang
- Matching sewing thread

MEASUREMENTS

The finished laundry bag measures 26 x 18 inches (65 x 45 cm).

MAKING THE LAUNDRY BAG

Step 1: Place the two gray outer pieces of fabric right sides together. Stitch down the side, along the bottom, and up the other side, using a ⅗-inch (1½-cm) seam allowance. Repeat with the two orange lining pieces, but leave a 4-inch (10-cm) gap along the bottom for turning. (Fig. 1)

Step 2: Place the outer bag, right side out, inside the lining bag, wrong sides out. Right sides should now be together. Match up the side seams. Stitch together all the way around the top. Turn the bag right side out through the gap in the lining. Slip-stitch the gap closed. (Fig. 2)

Step 3: Push the lining inside the outer bag and then topstitch around the bag opening, approximately ⅕ inch (½ cm) from the edge, to secure. (Fig. 3)

Step 4: Place the embroidery inner hoop over the outer bag and fold the top over it by approximately 1½ inches (4 cm). Place the outer hoop on top, over the lining. Tighten the screw to finish. (Fig. 4)

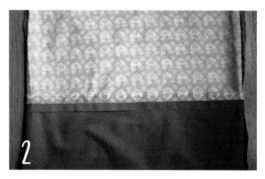

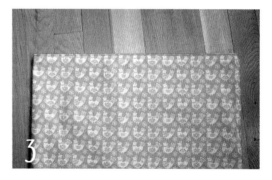

LAMPSHADE

If you prefer, you can glue your lampshade cover in place at the top and bottom instead of stitching it.

Use ribbon to add a colorful edge to your lampshade.

YOU WILL NEED

- Cotton fabric (see instructions for sizing)
- Drum lampshade
- Matching sewing thread
- Ribbon (see instructions for size)

MEASUREMENTS

To fit your lampshade

MAKING THE LAMPSHADE

Step 1: You will need a plain, fabric-covered lampshade and enough fabric to wrap around it. Measure the height and circumference of your lampshade and add 1¼ inches (approximately 3 cm) to both measurements. Cut out your fabric to this size. (Fig. 1)

Step 2: Wrap the fabric right side down around your lampshade and pin, right sides together, along the side to make sure it fits. (Fig. 2)

Step 3: Keeping your fabric pinned, ease it off the lampshade, and stitch together along the pinned line. (Fig. 3)

Step 4: Press the seam open. Fold the top and bottom edges ⅗ inch (1½ cm) to the wrong sides. Press. (Fig. 4)

Step 5: Turn the cover right side out and slip it over your lampshade. Secure it in place by making a small stitch through the edge of the fabric cover on the lampshade and the edge of your fabric cover. Stitch all the way around the top and bottom edges. (Fig. 5)

Step 6: Cut lengths of ribbon to fit around the top and bottom of the lampshade. Glue in place to finish. (Fig. 6)

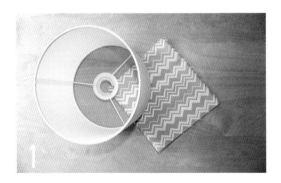

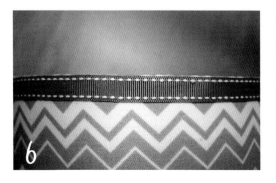

PILLOWCASE WITH TASSELS

We used cotton DK yarn for our tassels, but embroidery floss also works well. Experiment with different colors and weights of yarn and thread to get the effect you want.

Attach tassels to your pillowcase at regular intervals.

YOU WILL NEED

- Plain standard pillowcase, 20 x 30 inches (50 x 75 cm)
- Yarn or embroidery floss for tassels
- Cardboard, 4 x 4 inches (10 x 10 cm)
- Matching sewing thread

MEASUREMENTS

Each finished tassel measures 2 inches (5 cm) long.

MAKING EACH TASSEL

Step 1: Fold your piece of cardboard in half. Starting at the open side, wind your yarn around the cardboard approximately twenty times. (Fig. 1)

Step 2: Cut a piece of thread approximately 6 inches (15 cm) long. Thread it under the yarn wraps at the folded edge of the cardboard. Knot tightly twice. (Fig. 2)

Step 3: Insert scissors between the wraps at the cardboard's open side. Cut the yarn. (Fig. 3)

Step 4: Slide the yarn off the cardboard. Cut another piece of thread, approximately

6 inches (15 cm), and knot it around the yarn, approximately ⅖ inch (1 cm) down from the top. Wind one end around the knot a few times and then knot again twice. (Fig. 4)

Step 5: Pull the wound thread down to the bottom of the tassel. Trim all the yarn ends to the same length to neaten. (Fig. 5)

ATTACH EACH TASSEL

Step 6: Find the two ends that you tied around the top of your tassel and thread one onto a needle. Insert the needle into the edge of the pillowcase seam to the wrong side. Repeat with the other end a short distance away. Knot together to secure. Attach more tassels in the same way around the pillowcase. (Fig. 6)

FABRIC-MOUNTED PICTURE FRAME

We left the glass out of our frames so that we can enjoy the texture of the fabric, but you can include the glass if you prefer.

YOU WILL NEED

- Picture frame
- Cotton print fabric to fit frame
- Heavyweight interfacing to fit frame
- Double-sided tape

MAKING THE FRAME

Step 1: Remove the backing and glass from your frame and then place it over your piece of fabric until you are happy with the position of the pattern inside. Draw around the outside of the picture frame onto your fabric. (Fig. 1)

Step 2: Cut out your fabric, just inside the outline you drew. Iron heavyweight interfacing to the wrong side of your fabric. (Fig. 2)

Step 3: Using double-sided tape, attach your fabric to the paper inset that comes with the frame. Trim the fabric to fit, if needed. Place the fabric and inset into your frame and then place the backing board on top. (Fig. 3)

Step 4: Turn the frame over, and your fabric picture is now finished! (Fig. 4)

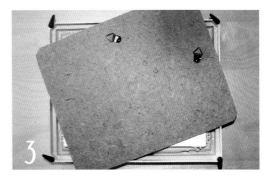

Get your fave fabrics out of your stash and frame them.

FRESH LOOKS

PROJECTS FOR THE SECOND-FLOOR ROOMS

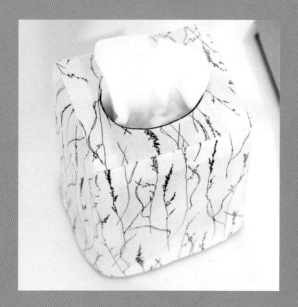

For the bedroom, bathroom, and landing, these projects will coordinate your second floor!

Designer: Rebecca Reid **Styling:** Louise Day **Photography:** Philip Sowels

FABRIC BOXES

Everyone needs storage—we just like ours to look good, especially when it's so easy to make your own. Whatever size boxes you choose, stack them in contrasting colors or patterns for impact and coordinate with complementary accessories.

AHH... TISSUES!

We never really like the designs on tissue boxes, whatever their shape, so we've made a simple cover for them. This idea makes a great gift, too, because everyone needs tissues.

Amber, Guinevere & Kate
photographed by Craig McDean   1995–2005

"LET'S MAKE STUFF" BANNER

Join in our mantra and sew yourself a decorative banner to hang anywhere you choose. Don't stop with a single message—make up your own for birthdays, anniversaries, and other special occasions.

BOLSTER AND BENCH CUSHIONS

Add some comfort and a little luxury with new cushions in any room. Bolster cushions make great head- or armrests on a window seat or as extra padding for bedtime reading. Our made-to-measure bench cushion, meanwhile, creates a cozy space for daytime lounging.

EMBELLISH A TOWEL

Plain towels made posh! Practice your patchwork skills by sewing each of the fabrics together to create an edging, or appliqué someone's initials on a bath towel.

TOILET-PAPER ROLL HOLDER

We're talking tasteful, stylish holders that will exude class and add a touch of elegance to the smallest room in the house.

FABRIC BOXES

Covered boxes make for stylish storage

YOU WILL NEED

- Outer fabric:
  Small: 23⅝ x 44 inches (60 x 12 cm)
  Medium: 39 x 44 inches (100 x 112 cm)
  Large: 63 x 44 inches (60 x 112 cm)
- Cotton lining fabric, cream:
  Small: 24 x 44 inches (60 x 112 cm)
  Medium: 39 x 44 inches (100 x 112 cm)
  Large: 63 x 44 inches (160 x 112 cm)
- White foam board:
  Small: One 17 x 24-inch (43 x 61 cm) sheet
  Medium: Three 17 x 24-inch (43 x 61 cm) sheets
  Large: Six 17 x 24-inch (43 x 61 cm) sheets
- Double-sided tape
- Matching sewing thread

MEASUREMENTS

Small box measures 7⅞ inches (20 cm)
Medium box measures 11⅞ inches (30 cm)
Large box measures 15¾ inches (40 cm)

Note: Use a ⅝-inch (1½-cm) seam allowance throughout and press all seams open as you go.

CUTTING

From the outer and lining fabric, cut:

- For the base and sides, five pieces of each:
  Small: 10¼ x 10¼ inches (26 x 26 cm)
  Medium: 14⅛ x 14⅛ inches (36 x 36 cm)
  Large: 18⅛ x 18⅛ inches (46 x 46 cm)
- For the lid top, one piece of each:
  Small: 10⅝ x 10⅝ inches (27 x 27 cm)
  Medium: 14⅝ x 14⅝ inches (37 x 37 cm)
  Large: 18½ x 18½ inches (47 x 47 cm)
- For the lid sides, four pieces of each:
  Small: 3⅛ x 10⅝ inches (8 x 27 cm)
  Medium: 3⅛ x 14⅝ inches (8 x 37cm)
  Large: 3⅛ x 18½ inches (8 x 47 cm)

From the foam board, cut:

- For the base and sides, five pieces:
  Small: 7⅞ x 7⅞ inches (20 x 20 cm)
  Medium: 11⅞ x 11⅞ inches (30 x 30 cm)
  Large: 15¾ x 15¾ inches (40 x 40 cm)
- For the lid top, one piece:
  Small: 8¼ x 8¼ inches (21 x 21 cm)
  Medium: 12¼ x 12¼ inches (31 x 31 cm)
  Large: 16⅛ x 16⅛ inches (41 x 41 cm)
- For the lid sides, four pieces:
  Small: 1⅝ x 8¼ inches (4 x 21 cm)
  Medium: 1⅝ x 12¼ inches (4 x 31 cm)
  Large: 1⅝ x 16⅛ inches (4 x 41 cm)

COVERING THE BOARD

Each of the storage boxes is assembled in the same way.

Step 1: Start by covering all of your foam board pieces in fabric. Place the outer fabric right side down and then center the corresponding piece of foam board on top. Stick strips of double-sided

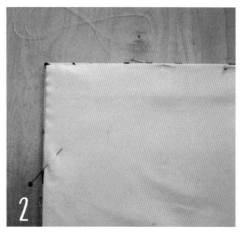

tape around all four sides close to the edge of the board and then fold the fabric edges over the board and press into place to hold them securely while you stitch them together. (Fig. 1)

Step 2: Place the corresponding lining piece right side up on top of the foam board over which you just folded the fabric. Turn the edges under so they meet up with the folded-over edges of the outer fabric. Slip-stitch the two fabric edges together all the way around, keeping your stitches neat and small. (Fig. 2)

Step 3: Cover and line each of the foam board pieces in the same way so that you have a total of ten pieces.

JOINING THE PIECES

Step 1: Take two of the side pieces and place them with the lining sides together. Work a few small stitches through the outer fabric at one end to anchor your thread and then oversew the two pieces together down the side. You should only stitch through the outer fabric, and you'll find it easier if you angle the pieces slightly so your stitches are neat and barely visible. (Fig. 3)

Step 2: Join the other side pieces together in the same way. (Fig. 4)

Step 3: Stitch the base to the bottom edges of the four sides to complete the bottom of the box. You may find it easier pin the corners in place before you start to keep them in place. (Fig. 5)

Step 4: Stitch the four lid sides together and then join the lid top to them. (Fig. 6)

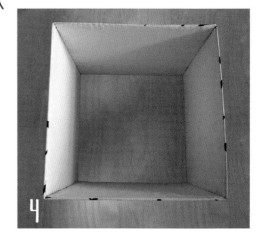

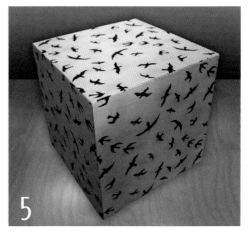

TISSUE-BOX COVER

YOU WILL NEED

- Outer fabric: see instructions for details
- Inner fabric: see instructions for details
- Tissue box
- Matching sewing thread

MEASUREMENTS

The finished tissue box cover will fit your tissue box.

Note: Use a ⅝-inch (1½-cm) seam allowance.

MEASURING

Step 1: To make a cover to fit any size tissue box, you first need to figure out the measurements of fabric to cut out.

Box top: Measure the top of the tissue box and add 1¼ inches (3 cm) to the width and to the length. Cut one piece each from the outer fabric and inner fabric.

Box sides: Measure each side of your tissue box and add 1¼ inches (3 cm) to the width and to the height. Cut one piece for each side from both the outer and inner fabrics.

MAKING THE TOP HOLE

Step 1: Place the box-top outer fabric wrong side up. Take the perforated cardboard oval out of the top of the tissue box, center it on the fabric, and then trace around it.

Step 2: Pin the box-top outer and inner fabric right sides together. Stitch together all around the drawn line. (Fig. 1)

Step 3: Cut through both layers of fabric ¼ inch (½ cm) inside the stitched line and then cut notches from the fabric. (Fig. 2)

Step 4: Turn the top right side out by pushing one piece through the hole and then press. (Fig. 3)

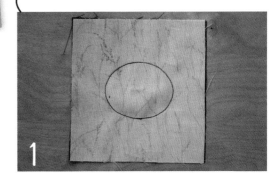

JOINING THE SIDES

Step 1: Starting ⅝ inch (1½ cm) down from the top edge but finishing at the bottom edge, stitch all of the side pieces together down the height with right sides together. Remember to join them in the correct order if your box is rectangular. By not stitching the top ⅝ inch (1½ cm) of the side seams, you'll find that the top fits more neatly into place later. Repeat with the inner fabric sides. (Fig. 4)

ATTACHING THE TOP

Step 1: Start by joining the outer top panel to the outer sides. Pin the inner top panel out of the way so it doesn't get caught in your stitching. (Fig. 5)

Step 2: Join the inner top to the inner side panels in the same way. (Fig. 6)

HEMMING THE LOWER EDGE

Step 1: Push the assembled inner fabric cover to inside the outer fabric cover.

Step 2: Turn the outer lower edge of the four sides under by ⅝ inch (1½ cm) and press. Repeat with the inner lower edges so they meet up with the turned-under outer lower edges. Topstitch all the way around to hem. (Fig. 7)

Step 3: Slip the cover over your tissue box to complete. It is reversible, so you can choose whichever side you prefer on the outside. (Fig. 8)

PATCHWORK TOWEL

Wash your towel before you add the border if it's new just to be sure the color doesn't run into your patchwork fabric.

YOU WILL NEED

- Cotton fabrics: see instructions for details
- Towel, navy blue
- Matching sewing thread

MEASUREMENTS

You can add a patchwork border to any size towel.

CUTTING THE FABRIC

Step 1: Each of the patchwork strips measure 1⅝ inches (4 cm) wide when sewn together. Measure across the width of your towel and then divide this measurement by 1⅝ inches (4 cm) to calculate how many strips you need.

Step 2: Using a variety of fabrics to create a patchwork effect, cut each strip to 2¾ x 4¾ inches (7 x 12 cm).

MAKING THE BORDER

Step 1: Join all of your strips with right sides together along the long edges to make one continuous strip that will fit across the width of your towel. Press all seams open. (Fig. 1)

Step 2: Cut the hem off the short end of your towel to reduce the bulk when you bind it with your patchwork strip.

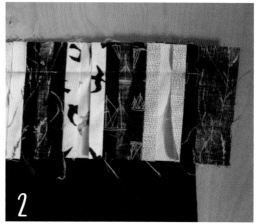

BINDING YOUR TOWEL

Step 1: Place the patchwork strip, right sides together, along the width of your towel, matching raw edges and making sure that the ends of the strip reach ⅝ inch (1½ cm) beyond the edges of the towel for turning later. Stitch the strip into place using a 1¼-inch (3-cm) seam allowance. (Fig. 2)

Step 2: Turn the strip over to the other side of the towel. Turn the long edge under by 1¼ inches (3 cm) so that the fold meets up with your line of stitching. Turn the short edges to the inside and press. Topstitch the border in place, making sure to stitch through the edge of the border strip at both the back and the front. (Fig. 3)

Step 3: Finish by hand-stitching the short ends together with small, neat stitches. (Fig. 4)

TOILET-PAPER-ROLL HOLDER

It's easy to adapt this project to fit smaller toilet-paper rolls. If the spaces are too big, work another line of stitching below the first in the gaps between each roll.

YOU WILL NEED

- Main fabric: 33 x 12 inches (85 x 30 cm)
- Lining fabric: 33 x 12 inches (85 x 30 cm)
- Twill tape, navy blue: 10 inches (25 cm)
- Matching sewing thread

MEASUREMENTS

The finished toilet-paper roll holder measures 32⅜ x 4¾ inches (82 x 12 cm).

Note: Use a ⅝-inch (1½-cm) seam allowance throughout and press all seams open as you go.

CUTTING THE FABRIC

Step 1: Cut the main fabric into two pieces, each measuring 33½ x 6 inches (85 x 15 cm).

Step 2: Cut the lining fabric into two pieces, each measuring 33½ x 6 inches (85 x 15 cm).

ASSEMBLING

Step 1: Place the two main pieces of fabric right sides together, matching raw edges. Stitch together along one short edge.

Step 2: Repeat with the two pieces of lining fabric. Open both main and lining pieces flat to make two long strips. (Fig. 1)

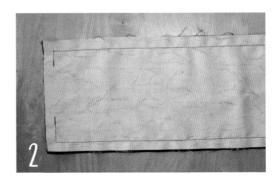

Step 3: Place the joined main and lining fabric right sides together and stitch around all four sides but leave a 3⅛-inch (8-cm) gap in the center of one short edge for turning. (Fig. 2)

Step 4: Turn the fabric right side out and fold the edges of the gap to the inside. Press.

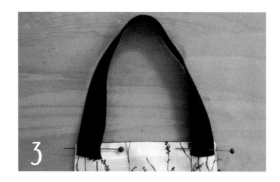

Step 5: Pin one end of the twill tape to the top of the lining, positioning the end of it ⅜ inch (1 cm) down from the top and just in from the side edge. Pin the other end of the tape to the other end of the top edge. (Fig 3)

Step 6: Fold the fabric in half with lining sides together, matching top edges. Stitch the two ends together, working one row ⅛ inch (2 mm) from the top and then the second row ¾ inch (2 cm) from the top. This will hold the hanging loop tape in place and join the fabrics together. (Fig. 4)

Step 7: Measure 8¾ inches (22 cm) down from the top short edges and mark this position with masking tape across the fabric. Measure 7⅞ inches (20 cm) down from this, mark with tape, and then measure a third line 7⅞ inches (20 cm) down from this. Pin the folded fabric together just above the tape to hold in place. Stitch alongside the top edges of the three pieces of tape. (Fig. 5)

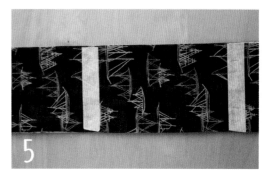

Step 8: Remove the masking tape and then slide your toilet-paper rolls in the spaces between each line of stitching. Hang on the wall using the loop at the top. (Fig. 6)

APPLIQUÉ TOWEL

YOU WILL NEED

- Cotton fabric: see instructions for details
- Fusible web: see instructions for details
- Towel, navy blue
- Matching sewing thread

MEASUREMENTS

You can appliqué an initial or motif on any size bath/hand towel.

APPLIQUÉING THE INITIAL

Step 1: Print out your initial in the font and size you want to stitch on your towel. There are many websites where you can download free fonts, or you can use a font already installed on your computer.

Step 2: Trace over the initial onto tracing paper. Turn it over to the wrong side and place the fusible web on top, paper side up. Now trace over the initial onto the paper side so that you are tracing it in reverse.

Step 3: Place your traced fusible web onto the wrong side of your cotton fabric, paper side up, and press it gently until it is firmly stuck in place.

Step 4: Carefully cut out the initial along your drawn pencil lines. (Fig. 1)

Step 5: Remove the paper backing from the initial and then position it right side up onto your towel in the position you want. Press carefully into place.

Step 6: Stitch around the initial using a machine zigzag stitch, working slowly and carefully so that the stitches reach just over the edge of the initial and onto the towel. (Fig. 2)

BOLSTER CUSHION

YOU WILL NEED

- Main fabric: 20 x 44 inches (50 x 112 cm)
- Piping and button fabric: 4 x 26 inches (8 x 65 cm)
- Piping cord: 48 inches (120 cm)
- Zipper: 16 inches (40 cm)
- Two 1¼-inch (30-mm) diameter self-cover buttons
- Bolster cushion pad: 18 x 7 inches (45 x 17 cm)

MEASUREMENTS

The finished bolster cushion cover measures 18 x 7 inches (45 x 17 cm).

Note: Use a ⅝-inch (1½-cm) seam allowance throughout and press all seams open.

CUTTING OUT

Step 1: Cut the main fabric into the following pieces:

- For the main cushion body:
  18⅞ x 22⅛ inches (48 x 56 cm)
- For the cushion ends: two pieces
  4¾ x 22⅛ inches (12 x 56 cm) each

Step 2: Cut the piping fabric into the following pieces:

- For the piping strips: two pieces
  1⅝ x 23⅝ inches (4 x 60 cm) each
- For the button covers: two pieces
  2 x 2 inches (5 x 5 cm)

INSERTING THE ZIPPER

Step 1: Fold the main cushion body in half lengthwise with the right sides together and then stitch a 2-inch (5-cm) seam from either end. Work a row of tacking stitches between the side seams, again with a seam allowance of ⅝ inches (1½ cm). (Fig. 1)

Step 2: Open the joined fabric pieces and, right side down, press the stitched and tacked seam open. Place your zipper right side down over the tacked gap between the seams and pin it into place. Using a zipper foot, stitch the zipper into place close to the teeth and then remove the tacking stitches. (Fig. 2)

ADDING THE COVERED PIPING

Step 1: Cut the piping cord in half and cover each length with the two piping strips of fabric

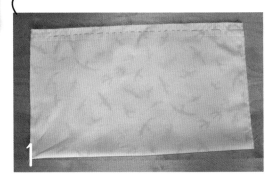

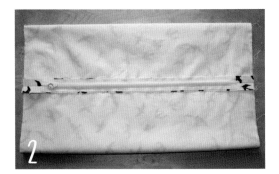

in the same way as you did with the bench cushion.

Step 2: Working at one end of the main cushion body, tack the covered piping cord all the way around. Line up the raw edges and clip the piping strip at intervals so it curves around neatly. Trim and join the ends as you did for the bench cushion and then repeat at the other end of the main cushion body.

ASSEMBLING THE COVER

Step 1: Take one cushion end strip and stitch the short ends right sides together. Repeat for the other end strip. (Fig. 4)

Step 2: Pin one joined cushion end, right sides together, on top of one end of the main cushion body, sandwiching the covered piping between them. Stitch together close to the piping. Repeat for the other end. (Fig. 5)

Step 3: Working on one end of the cushion, turn the long raw edge under by 1 inch (2½ cm) to the wrong side. (Fig. 6)

Step 4: Using a strong cotton thread, work a running stitch on the right side about ¼ inch (½ cm) up from the folded-under edge. Secure the thread tightly where you start and then work a couple of stitches past this to finish. Pull the thread up to gather the end and then secure. Repeat at the other end of the cushion. (Fig. 7)

Step 5: Cover the two self-cover buttons with your fabric squares and then stitch over the gathered ends of the bolster cushion to neaten and decorate. (Fig. 8)

BENCH CUSHION

Make this into a bench cushion for your garden by using a water-resistant fabric or canvas.

YOU WILL NEED

- Main fabric: 95 x 44 inches (240 x 112 cm)
- Piping fabric: 9½ x 44 inches (24 x 112 cm)
- Piping cord: 178 inches (4½ m)
- Zip: 39 inches (1 m)
- Foam insert: 44½ x 18 x 4 inches (113 x 45 x 10 cm)
- Matching sewing thread

MEASUREMENTS

The finished bench cover measures 44½ x 17¾ x 4 inches (113 x 45 x 10 cm).

FOAM

We used a premium upholstery foam that will hold its shape, making it ideal for a bench or window-seat cushion. Look for a retailer who will cut foam to your exact requirements so you can make cushions of any size and shape you want.

Note: Use a ⅝-inch (1½-cm) seam allowance throughout and press all seams open as you go.

CUTTING THE FABRIC

Step 1: Cut the main fabric into the following pieces:

- For the top and bottom: two pieces 18⅞ x 45½ inches (48 x 116 cm) each
- Front gusset: 5¼ x 45½ inches (13 x 116 cm)
- Side gussets: two pieces 5¼ x 18⅞ inches (13 x 48 cm) each
- Back gussets: two pieces 3⅛ x 45½ inches (8 x 116 cm) each

Step 2: Cut the piping fabric into six strips 1⅝ x 44 inches (4 x 112 cm) each.

MAKING THE COVERED PIPING

Step 1: Take two of the piping strips, place them right sides together at right angles, and stitch them together diagonally. Trim the seam, open, and press. (Fig. 1)

Step 2: Join all six strips together in the same way to make one long strip.

Step 3: Fold the joined piping strip wrong sides together around the piping cord and stitch the raw edges just ⅜ inch (1 cm) from the edge to ensure that these stitches won't show later. (Fig. 2)

Step 4: Trim each corner of the top and bottom fabrics to make them slightly rounded, which will help the piping ease around more smoothly.

Step 5: Take the top fabric and, starting in the center of the long side, which will be at the back, tack the covered piping cord all the way around the edge. Be sure to line up the raw edges and clip the piping strip at the corners so it curves around neatly. Trim the end so it overlaps the start by 2 inches (5 cm). (Fig. 3)

Step 6: Trim and join the two short ends of the fabric to fit together exactly. Splice the cord by removing half of the strands from each end and then winding them together for a neat joint. Tack the joined piping strip around the cord and to the cushion-top fabric. (Fig. 4)

Step 7: Repeat this whole process to attach covered piping all around the edge of the cushion-bottom fabric.

INSERTING THE ZIPPER

Step 1: Take the two back gusset pieces, place them right sides together, and then, along one

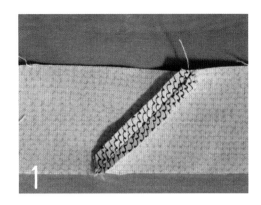

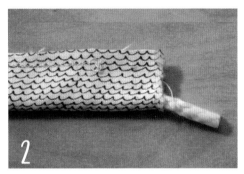

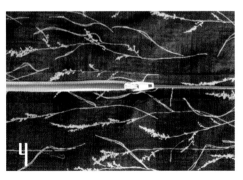

long edge, stitch a 4-inch (10-cm) seam from either end. Work a row of tacking stitches between these side seams, again using a ⅝-inch (1½-cm) seam allowance, then press the stitched and tacked seam open. (Fig. 5)

Step 2: Place your zipper right side down over the wrong side of the tacked gap between the seams and pin into place. Using a zipper foot, stitch the zipper into place close to the teeth. (Fig. 6)

ASSEMBLING THE COVER

Step 1: Join the four gusset strips together along the short edges to make one continuous piece. Do this by joining a short side piece to the back piece with the zipper inserted, then another short side piece, and then the long front piece. Start and finish each seam ⅝ inch (1½ cm) from each end; this will help the gusset lie flatter when you join it to the top and bottom cushion pieces.

Step 2: Join the assembled gusset to the top of the cushion with covered piping attached. Starting at one end of the long back gusset piece and back long edge of the piped top pieces, stitch right sides together close to the piping. (Fig. 7)

Step 3: Pivot your sewing machine needle at each corner and continue stitching the gusset all the way around the top of the cushion piece.

Step 4: Open up the zipper in the gusset back piece and then join the gussets, right sides together, to the piped cushion bottom piece in the same way.

Step 5: Turn your cover right side out and press. Put your foam inside your cushion cover and close the zipper to complete. (Fig. 8)

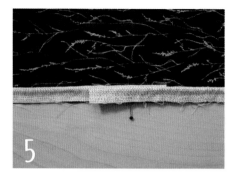

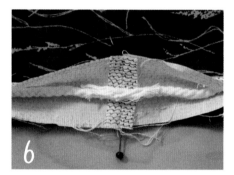

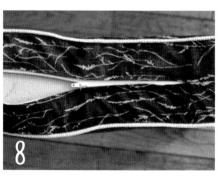

BANNER

YOU WILL NEED

- Main fabric: 24 x 17 inches (60 x 43 cm)
- Backing and appliqué fabric:
  24 x 26 inches (60 x 65 cm)
- Interlining: 24 x 17 inches (60 x 43 cm)
- Fusible web: 13 x 9 inches (32 x 22 cm)
- Wooden dowel: ½ x 18 inches
  (1½ x 46 cm)
- Twill tape
- Matching sewing thread

MEASUREMENTS

Banner measures 20 x 16 inches (50 x 40 cm).

Note: Use a ⅝-inch (1½-cm) seam allowance.

CUTTING THE FABRIC

   Step 1: Cut your main fabric into a point to make the banner shape, following the measurements on the diagram on page 220.

   Step 2: Cut the backing fabric to the same shape as the main fabric. You will use the remainder for your appliqué.

APPLIQUÉ

Step 1: Trace the words "LET'S MAKE STUFF," which you'll find as a printable sheet at *www.simplysewingmag.com/101ideas*. Turn it over to the wrong side and place your fusible web on top, paper side up. Now trace over the letters onto the paper side so you're tracing them in reverse. We spaced the apostrophe apart to make it easier to cut out. (Fig. 1)

Step 2: Place your traced fusible web paper side up onto the wrong side of your letters fabric and press gently into place using a dry, medium-temperature iron (don't use any steam) until it is firmly stuck.

Step 3: Carefully cut out all of the letters along your drawn pencil lines. Be sure to cut them accurately to create neat shapes. Remove the paper backing from the letters, and then you are ready to stick them in place.

Step 4: Place your main banner fabric right side up and then place all of the letters on top, centering each word across the fabric. The top of "LET'S" should be 6 inches (15 cm) from the top of the fabric. Press the letters carefully into place. (Fig. 2)

Step 4: Stitch around each letter by machine or hand to hold them firmly in place and for a decorative effect. (Fig. 3)

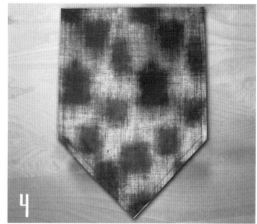

MAKING THE BANNER

Step 1: Cut the interlining into the same shape as the main banner. The interlining is used to give the banner a little more body so it hangs better. You can use a heavy cotton fabric, quilt batting, or fleece fabric.

Step 2: Place the main fabric right sides together with the backing fabric, and the interlining beneath the two. Stitch together, making sure to leave a 4-inch (10-cm) gap in the center of the top for turning. (Fig. 4)

Step 3: Turn the fabric right side out and press, and then topstitch all the way around to neaten and to close the gap at the top. (Fig. 5)

Step 4: Fold the top over by 2 inches (5 cm) to the back. Slip-stitch down to make a casing; be sure to only stitch through the lining. Thread the dowel through and then tie twill tape to either end for hanging the banner. (Fig. 6)

COZY
COVER-UP

No matter the season, every home
needs a hot-water-bottle cover!

By Jennie Jones

Make this fabulous cozy with just one fat quarter (approximately 18 x 22 inches [46 x 56 cm]) of your favorite fabric!

HOT-WATER-BOTTLE COVER

YOU WILL NEED

- 1 fat quarter, approximately 18 x 22 inches (46 x 56 cm)
- Lining fabric, fat quarter, approximately 18 x 22 inches (46 x 56 cm)
- Piping cord, 80 inches (2 m)
- Bias binding, 80 inches (2 m)
- Vintage button
- Matching sewing thread
- Basic sewing kit

Step 1: Make a template approximately 1 inch (2½ cm) larger than your hot-water bottle. (Fig. 1) Pin the template to your fabric and cut out the front panel. To cut out the bottom back panel, use the same template, but cut straight across two-thirds of the way up. To create the top back panel, again use the front panel template, and ensure it will overlap the bottom back panel by around 2 inches (5 cm). (Fig. 2)

Use these pieces as templates to cut the lining to the same sizes. (Fig. 3)

Step 2: You will need approximately 60 inches (1½ m) of piping and binding for the outside edges and the opening on the back. Open your bias binding, wrap it around the piping, and sew, taking care not to get too close to the cord. (Fig. 4)

With the remaining binding, make a loop for the button and a bow. (Fig. 5)

Step 3: Place the top back panel right side up. Pin the covered piping along the bottom edge. Place the loop at the center of the bottom edge, pin the lining on top, and sew into place close to the cord. (Fig. 6)

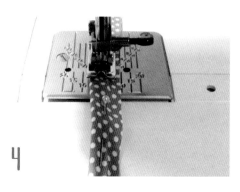

Sew the top back panel to the lining with wrong sides together using a zigzag stitch around the edges. Repeat with the bottom back panel and lining, turning the top edges under to hem. Place the two back pieces right sides up with the top back panel overlapping the bottom back panel in preparation for sewing them to the front panel. (Fig. 7)

Step 4: Zigzag-stitch the front panel and front lining wrong sides together. Pin the piping around the right side of the front panel and sew close to the cord. At one end, cut the cord inside, fold the bias in, and then sew the other end of the piping inside. (Fig. 8)

Step 5: Clip the curves. (Fig. 9)
Stitch the front panel to the back panels, right sides together, close to the piping. Turn right side out. Sew on the bow and the button. (Fig. 10)

PRETTY IN PINK

PASTEL SHADES FOR A RELAXING BEDROOM

Soft pastel pinks and grays create
a cool, calming bedroom—the
perfect place to relax!

Designer: Rebecca Reid Styling: Lisa Jones Photography: Jesse Wild

CHILL-OUT ZONE

Create the ultimate chill-out corner with this comfy beanbag chair, made from two gorgeous (and durable) canvas fabrics. Make one for the living room, too!

TRINKET TRAYS

Keep special items safe and sound in these candy-hued fabric trays. They're easy to put together and would be a fab gift for a jewelry-loving friend.

PASTEL BEDROOM

HANG IT UP

Cover plain wire hangers with matching fabrics for a coordinated, pulled-together look—perfect for hanging up this soft flannel kimono (you can find the kimono pattern in issue 7 of *Simply Sewing:* *www.simplysewingmag.com*).

GOT IT COVERED

Doodles aren't the only way to personalize your notebooks! These fabric-covered notebooks look pretty and decorative huddled together on the shelf, and the notebooks inside can be easily replaced as needed.

BED RUNNER

YOU WILL NEED

- Top fabric: 28 x 44 inches (70 x 112 cm)
- Backing fabric: 32 x 44 inches (80 x 112 cm)
- Binding fabric: 13 x 44 inches (32 x 112 cm)
- Cotton quilt batting: 18 x 67 inches (45 x 170 cm)
- Matching sewing thread
- Basic sewing kit

MEASUREMENTS

The finished runner measures 13¾ x 63 inches (35 x 160 cm).

BATTING USED

We used a 100-percent natural cotton batting with scrim, which is available in precut pieces or by the yard (meter). Cotton batting is very soft and drapes well, so it is perfect for a bed runner. It also has the benefit of being machine washable once the project is finished, but it's best to hand-wash it before you start to allow for shrinkage.

Note: Use a ⅝-inch (1½-cm) seam allowance and press all seams open as you go.

CUTTING THE FABRIC

Step 1: Cut the top fabric into a center section measuring 13¾ x 36⅝ inches (35 x 93 cm) and two side sections, each measuring 13¾ x 14⅜ inches (35 x 36 ½ cm) Be sure to cut the side sections so the pattern matches up with the center section when you join them together. You may need to buy extra fabric to do this.

Step 2: Cut the backing fabric into a center section measuring 17¾ x 36⅝ inches (45 x 93 cm) and two side sections, each measuring 17¾ x 17¾ inches (45 x 45 cm).

JOINING THE FABRIC PIECES

Step 1: Take one side section and place it right sides together on top of the left side of the center section, matching raw edges. Stitch together down the short side. (Fig. 1)

Step 2: With right sides together, place the other side section on top of the central section's opposite side and stitch together as in Step 1.

Step 3: Join the three backing pieces together in the same way.

QUILTING THE BED RUNNER

Step 1: The backing fabric and batting are slightly larger than the top fabric to allow for any shrinkage or movement during quilting; you will trim them before you bind your bed runner. Place the backing fabric right side down, then place the batting on top of it, and finally place the joined top fabric right side up on top to make a sandwich.

Step 2: Tack all three layers together in a grid formation, starting from the center and working outward to join them together securely. Be sure to also tack all the way around the edge to hold it in place when you attach your binding later. (Fig. 2)

Step 3: You can quilt your bed runner in whatever pattern you prefer. Simple squares look nice, or you could quilt around some of the printed patterns on the fabric. We quilted our bed runner in two parallel rows along the length of the runner and then worked diagonal lines spaced 4¾ inches (12 cm) apart across the parallel rows. A very simple way of doing this is to stick strips of masking tape on top of the fabric in the position you want your quilting to be. You can then quilt your line right up to the tape. Once you've finished stitching a line, simply remove the tape, and you'll have a neat row of quilting.

You can quilt either by machine or by hand. If you want to quilt by machine, simply stitch through all three layers, following the edge of the tape. To quilt by hand, use quilting thread and work a row of small running stitches through all three layers alongside the edge of the masking tape. With a little practice, you will be able to work several stitches at a time. (Fig. 3)

Step 4: When you have finished quilting all of the lines in one direction, remove the tape, stick more tape in the opposite direction, and quilt along these lines to create your pattern.

Step 5: When you are finished quilting, trim the backing and batting so that it lines up with the edge of the top and leaves a nice, crisp edge. Remove any frayed threads.

BINDING THE EDGES

Step 1: Take two of the binding strips, place them right sides together at right angles, and stitch them together diagonally. Trim the seam, open it out, and press. (Fig. 4)

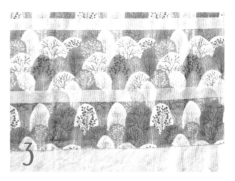

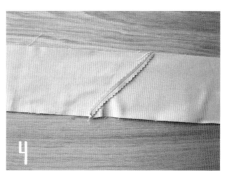

Step 2: Join all four strips together in the same way to make one long strip.

Step 3: Fold your long binding strip in half lengthwise with wrong sides together.

Step 4: Place the short end of your folded binding strip on top of the center of one short side of your runner, matching the raw edges. Turn the short end over by ⅜ inch (1 cm) and pin into place. Sew the binding to the runner using a ⅜-inch (1-cm) seam allowance.

Step 5: Stop stitching when you are ⅜ inch (1 cm) from the corner, reverse-stitch to secure, and then remove from your machine. (Fig. 5)

Step 6: Fold the binding so that it is at a 90 degree angle to the quilt top, making sure that the edge of the quilt and binding run in a straight line. (Fig. 6)

Step 7: Now fold the binding back down, aligning the sides and the top edge, and pin into place down the next side.

Step 8: Start stitching at the top edge and then stitch the binding in place all the way down. Stop ⅜ inch (1 cm) from the next corner and repeat this folding and turning process. (Fig. 7)

When you reach the point where you started, overlap over the turned over end by ¾ inch (2 cm), trim the excess, and stitch in place.

Step 9: Turn the binding over to the back of your runner and fold the corners into a mitered point. Slip-stitch the binding into place by hand or topstitch by machine if you prefer. (Fig. 8)

Step 10: Remove all tacking stitches to complete.

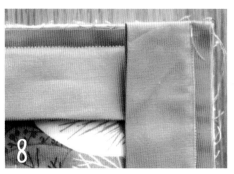

CLOUD CUSHIONS

YOU WILL NEED

- Large cloud fabric: 16 x 44 inches
  (40 x 112 cm)
- Small cloud fabric: 14 x 44 inches
  (35 x 112 cm)
- Polyester fiberfill
- Matching sewing thread
- Basic sewing kit

MEASUREMENTS

The large cushion measures 14⅝ x 19¾ inches
(37 x 50 cm). The small cloud measures
11 x 15 inches (28 x 38 cm).

Notes: Use a ⅝-inch (1½-cm) seam allowance
and press all seams open as you go.
You'll find both cloud templates (plus a bonus
extra-large size) online from *Simply Sewing*:
www.simplysewingmag.com/101ideas.

CUTTING OUT

Step 1: Trace around the printed-out
template for whichever cloud size you want to
make and then cut it out.

Step 2: Fold your fabric piece in half
widthwise with right sides together and then
pin your template on top, centered. Draw

around the template and then cut through both layers of fabric ⅝ inch (1½ cm) outside the line all the way around the drawn line. (Fig. 1)

STITCHING THE CUSHION

Step 1: Pin the two layers of fabric together, keeping the right sides facing. Stitch the two pieces together, starting 2 inches (5 cm) from the center of the bottom edge.

Step 2: Stitch the two layers together all the way around, finishing 2 inches (5 cm) from the center point to leave a 4-inch (10-cm) gap for turning and stuffing the cushion. (Fig. 2)

Step 3: Clip notches in all of the curves to help the fabric lie flat. Press the seam open. (Fig. 3)

Step 4: Turn your cloud right side out and press, being sure to press the excess fabric at the edges of the gap through to the inside of the cushion.

Step 5: Stuff your cushion fairly firmly, pushing stuffing into all of the curves to give a nice, rounded shape.

Step 6: Slip-stitch the gap closed. (Fig. 4)

BEANBAG

YOU WILL NEED

- Main fabric: 32 x 44 inches (81 x 112 cm)
- Contrast fabric: 32 x 44 inches (81 x 112 cm)
- Zipper: 18 inches (46 cm) to match fabric
- Polystyrene beanbag filler: 4.5 cubic feet (130 liters)
- Matching sewing thread
- Basic sewing kit

MEASUREMENTS

The finished beanbag measures 43 x 30 inches (109 x 78 cm).

Note: Use a ⅝-inch (1½-cm) seam allowance and press all seams open as you go.

ASSEMBLING THE PIECES

Step 1: Place your two fabric pieces right sides facing and then stitch together along the two long edges. Work another line of stitching ¼ inch (5 mm) inside the first to strengthen your seam and help prevent the filler from coming out. Finish the fabric edges by either cutting with pinking shears or with a machine zigzag stitch to stop them from fraying.

Step 2: Fold the two joined pieces in half lengthwise, matching the raw stitched edges.

Step 3: Cut one short end into a curve to create the curved bottom edge of the seat. To do this, make a pencil mark 6 inches (15 cm) in from the right-hand side at the top. Draw a curved line from this mark to the bottom right-hand corner and then cut along this line. (Fig. 1)

Step 4: Unfold the fabric but leave this edge unstitched for now.

BEANBAG CONTINUED

INSERTING THE ZIPPER

Step 1: Take the opposite unstitched short end and open it up. Refold this end so that the side seams match and the fabrics remain right sides together and then press.

Step 2: Measure 6 inches (15 cm) in from each end and mark with a pin. Stitch up to the pin marks from each end, leaving a gap in the middle.

Step 3: Stitch the central seam between the two side seams by either using a long machine stitch or tacking by hand; you will stitch the zipper into this gap and will need to remove these stitches once you insert the zipper. (Fig. 2)

Step 4: Press the seams open and place as flat as you can, wrong side up. Pin the zipper right side down, centered over the central seam, and then stitch it into place from the wrong side. You may find it easier to tack the zipper in place before you stitch it. Remove the tacking stitches between the two seams and undo the zipper. (Fig. 3)

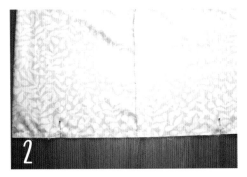

FINISHING

Step 1: Pin the curved edges (that you cut earlier) together. Create a double seam by stitching another line of machine stitching ¼ inch (5 mm) in toward the fabric edges from the first one. Finish the edges in the same way that you joined the two pieces of fabric together at the beginning. (Fig. 4)

Step 2: Turn your beanbag right side out and press all the seams.

Step 3: Pour in your beans and close the zip to complete.

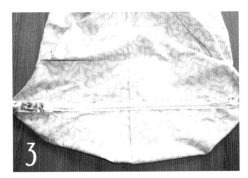

COVERED NOTEBOOKS

YOU WILL NEED

- Basic sewing kit

Large Notebook

- Outer fabric: 11 x 18 inches (26 x 46 cm)
- Lining fabric: 11 x 18 inches (26 x 46 cm)
- Quilt batting: 11 x 18 inches (26 x 46 cm)
- Narrow elastic: 12 inches (30 cm)
- A5 notebook: $5^4/_5$ x $8^3/_{10}$ inches (148 x 210 mm)
- Matching sewing thread

Small Notebook

- Outer fabric: 8 x 15 inches (20 x 37 cm)
- Lining fabric: 8 x 15 inches (20 x 37 cm)
- Quilt batting: 8 x 15 inches (20 x 37 cm)
- Narrow elastic: 10 inches (25 cm)
- A6 notebook: $4^1/_{10}$ x $5^4/_5$ inches (105 x 148 mm)
- Matching sewing thread

Note: Use a $5/_8$-inch (1-½ cm) seam allowance throughout and press all seams open as you go.

Step 1: These notebook covers are made with the same method no matter the size you are making. To begin, place the outer fabric right side up and then mark 4 inches (10 cm) for the A5 notebook or $3^5/_8$ inches (9 cm) for the A6 notebook from the left short side at the top and bottom with a pin. Tack the ends of the elastic at these points so that it lies flat on the fabric and then knot the ends to strengthen it. This will prevent it from pulling through the machine stitches when you sew it in place later. (Fig. 1)

Step 2: Place the outer fabric right side up on top of the batting and then place the lining fabric right side down on top of the outer fabric. The batting will give your book a soft, padded appearance, but you can leave the batting out if you prefer.

Step 3: Starting on the left short edge, stitch the fabrics and batting together all the way around but leave a 3⅛-inch (8-cm) gap in the center of the left side for turning. When you reach the elastic sandwiched between the fabrics, reverse stitch over it to strengthen the seam and to make sure it doesn't come out later.

Step 4: Clip the corners and then turn the book cover right side out. (Fig. 2)

Tuck in the excess fabric at the gap, press, and then slip-stitch the opening closed.

Step 5: Fold the fabric cover, centered, around your book with the flaps on the inside of the book cover. Pin the cover into place at the top and bottom so that it fits snugly and then remove the book.

Step 6: Topstitch along the long top and bottom edges to hold the flaps in place as well as to neaten the edges. Hold the elastic out of the way as you stitch to make sure you don't sew through it. (Fig. 3)

Step 7: Slip your notebook's front and back covers into the flaps and put the elastic over the front to hold your notebook closed. (Fig. 4)

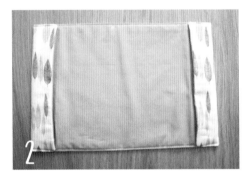

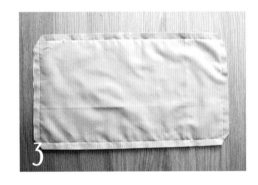

STORAGE TRAYS

YOU WILL NEED

- Basic sewing kit

Large Tray

- Outer fabric: 13 x 13 inches (33 x 33 cm)
- Lining fabric: 13 x 13 inches (33 x 33 cm)
- Foam board: 8 x 16 inches (20 x 40 cm)
- Matching sewing thread

Medium Tray

- Outer fabric: 10¼ x 10¼ inches (26 x 26 cm)
- Lining fabric: 10¼ x 10¼ inches (26 x 26 cm)
- Foam board: 6 x 12⅕ inches (15 x 31 cm)
- Matching sewing thread

Small Tray

- Outer fabric: 7½ x 7½ inches (19 x 19 cm)
- Lining fabric: 7½ x 7½ inches (19 x 19 cm)
- Foam board: 4 x 9 inches (10 x 22 cm)
- Matching sewing thread

MEASUREMENTS

The large tray measures 7⅞ x 7⅞ inches (20 x 20 cm). The medium tray measures 6 x 6 inches (15 x 15 cm). The small tray measures 4 x 4 inches (10 x 10 cm).

Note: Use a ⅝-inch (1½-cm) seam allowance throughout and press all seams open as you go.

Step 1: Cut the foam board into the following sizes. These pieces are used to give your storage tray structure.

Large Tray
Base: 7⅞ x 7⅞ inches (20 x 20 cm)
Sides: 4 pieces: 2 x 7⅞ inches (5 x 20 cm)

Medium Tray
Base: 6 x 6 inches (15 x 15 cm)
Sides: 4 pieces: 1⅝ x 6 inches (4 x 15 cm)

Small Tray
Base: 4 x 4 inches (10 x 10 cm)
Sides: 4 pieces: 1¼ x 4 inches (3 x 10 cm)

Step 2: All three sizes of tray are made in the same way. Start by turning one side of the outer fabric under by ⅝ inch (1½ cm) and press. Repeat by turning one edge under on the lining fabric.

Step 3: Place the outer and lining fabrics right sides together, making sure the turned-over edges are touching, and stitch together around the three sides that aren't turned over. Turn the fabric right side out and press. (Fig. 1)

Step 4: To make it easier to stitch the channels for inserting the foam board in the correct positions, draw these lines using an erasable pen or tack them on the right side of your outer fabric before you assemble the storage tray.

Step 5: Mark a vertical line all the way down the fabric as follows: large tray, 2 inches (5 cm) in from the left-hand side; medium tray, 1⅝ inches (4 cm) in from the left-hand side; small tray, 1¼ inches (3 cm) in from the left-hand side.

Step 6: Mark another vertical line the same distance from the right-hand side of the fabric.

Step 7 Turn your fabric around by 90 degrees and repeat this exactly, marking another two lines to make a grid. (Fig. 2)

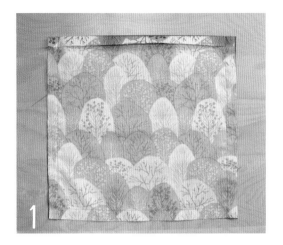

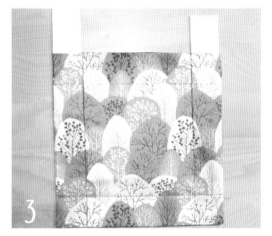

Step 8: With the open ends of the fabric facing toward you, stitch the two vertical lines by stitching through both layers of fabric. Use the marked lines to keep your stitching straight.

Step 9: Slip one side piece of foam board between the stitched lines so it sits at the opposite end of the fabric; it will fit quite snugly. Next, stitch the horizontal line to hold it in place. Slip the two side pieces and then the base piece in and stitch the two horizontal lines to hold them in place. (Fig. 3)

Step 10: Finally, slip the top side piece of foam board in and then slip-stitch the open sides closed to hold it in place.

Step 11: To assemble one corner, fold the sides up and then fold the corner fabric into a triangle point and stitch together down the side. Use the same thread that you used to stitch the channels and work small backstitches on top of the already worked machine stitches. Repeat with the other three corners to complete. (Fig. 4)

COAT HANGERS

YOU WILL NEED

- Cotton fabric: see instructions for details
- Wire coat hanger, white
- Matching sewing thread
- Basic sewing kit

Note: Use a ⅝-inch (1½-cm) seam allowance throughout and press all seams open as you go.

MEASURING

Step 1: Measure the length and height of your coat hanger (not including the hook). Cut two pieces of fabric that are each 4 inches (10 cm) longer than the coat hanger length and 4 inches (10 cm) wider than the height.

Step 2: Place one piece of fabric wrong side up, center your coat hanger on top of the fabric, and draw around it lightly in pencil. Draw another line ¾ inch (2 cm) outside the line you just traced at the top and sides and 2 inches (5 cm) below the bottom edge. Cut out your fabric along the outer line. (Fig. 1)

Step 3: Place the cut fabric right side down on top of the other piece of fabric, pin together within the drawn lines, and cut around it to make two shapes the same size.

Step 4: Measure and mark in pencil the center of the top of the cut fabric. Now measure and mark 1 inch (2½ cm) on each side of your center mark to make a 2-inch (5-cm) gap at the top (this is where you will thread the coat-hanger hook through later).

STITCHING THE COVER

Step 1: Stitch the two fabric pieces together down the angled edges and short sides, starting at the ends of the marked 2-inch (5-cm) gap for each side. (Fig. 2)

Step 2: Keeping the fabric wrong side out, turn the top opening between the seams under by ⅝ inch (1½ cm) and then turn the raw edge under this to make a double hem. Topstitch into place to neaten the top gap. (Fig. 3)

Step 3: Turn the bottom edges of the front and back fabrics under by ¾ inch (2 cm) and press. Turn the fabrics right sides out and press flat.

Step 4: Slip your coat hanger inside the cover, thread the hook through the gap at the top, and then pin the turned-under lower edges together and topstitch to complete. (Fig. 4)

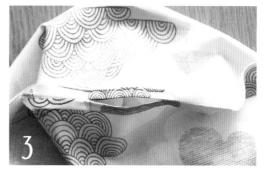

TIME TO PLAY

NURSERY TOYS AND DECORATIONS

Stitch tactile toys for a child's room to spark imagination and encourage indoor play.

Designer: Rebecca Reid **Styling:** Lisa Jones **Photography:** Philip Sowels

PADDED STOOL COVERS

Drawing, painting, hosting imaginary tea parties... the playroom table is where all the fun happens, so a comfy seat is a must! These fabric stool covers are simple to sew and can be personalized using embroidery or appliqué.

GEOMETRIC BUNTING

Brighten up the playroom or bedroom with bunting made from geometric shapes. Your child will have fun learning the names of the shapes, and you'll love how easy they are to make!

JIGSAW CUSHIONS

Stitch these jumbo jigsaw cushions in colorful fabrics for fun soft play. We've made four, but you could easily stitch more to form a huge floor cushion or make a complete puzzle by sewing straight outside edges.

DRAW-CORD PLAY MAT

Tidying up after playtime will be easy with this clever draw-cord play mat. When you pull its cord, the play mat transforms into a handy toy storage bag, which you can hang up out of the way or take with you.

KITE HEIGHT CHART

Children love to see how much they've grown. This keepsake kite height chart with a tape measure tail will save you from marking your walls or door frames. Simply glue a colorful felt shape onto a peg for each child and peg them onto the kite tail.

GEOMETRIC BUNTING

This technique works really well with paper shapes, too. Cut them out and machine-stitch for a fast finish.

YOU WILL NEED

- Cotton fabrics: 2⅜ x 4¾ inches (6 x 12 cm) for each shape
- Pinking shears
- Matching sewing thread
- Basic sewing kit

Note: You will find the templates needed to make this project on page 221.

MAKING THE SHAPES

Step 1: Trace around the templates and cut them out.

Step 2: To make each shape, cut your fabric in half to make two squares and then place them wrong sides together.

Step 3: Place one template in the center of one side of the fabric and draw around it. (Fig. 1)

Step 4: Stitch the two pieces of fabric together along the drawn lines.

Step 5: Cut out the shapes just outside the stitched line, using pinking shears for a decorative effect. You could use ordinary scissors instead if you prefer or alternate between some straight-edged and some pinked shapes. (Fig. 2)

Step 6: Lay all your shapes out on a flat surface and move them around until you are happy with the order of the colors and shapes. You can either alternate them

regularly or go for a more random selection. Pile up the shapes in the order you want them to be joined.

SEWING THE SHAPES TOGETHER

Step 1: Set your machine to a long, straight stitch (4 is about right).

Step 2: Make sure there is a long length of thread coming out of your machine because you'll need it to tie the bunting. Sew through the center of the first shape while holding onto the thread behind it tightly. (Fig. 3)

Step 3: When you have sewn through the first shape, continue sewing, again holding the shape and thread behind it tightly or the machine will become tangled because there is nothing for it to sew though.

Step 4: After a few stitches, feed the next shape from your pile through the machine and then continue adding all of the shapes in the same way. (Fig. 4)

Step 4: Leave a long length of thread at the end for tying when you have attached the final shape.

KITE HEIGHT CHART

YOU WILL NEED

- Main fabric: 14 x 24 inches (35 x 60 cm)
- Contrast fabric: 10 x 8 inches (25 x 20 cm)
- Kite tail fabric: 8 x 44 inches (20 x 112 cm)
- Heavyweight interfacing: 16 x 12 inches (40 x 30 cm)
- Ribbon: ¼ x 40 inches (5 mm x 1 m)
- Fabric tape measure: 60 inches (150 cm)
- Felt: For bows, see instructions for details
- Wooden pegs
- Matching sewing thread
- Basic sewing kit

Notes: Use a ⅜-inch (1 cm) seam allowance unless otherwise stated.

You will find the template at *www.simplysewingmag.com/101ideas*—just download and print it.

CUTTING THE FABRIC

Step 1: Trace the kite shape from the downloaded pattern. To make the individual kite shapes, trace each of the four triangles (A, B, C, D) separately and then draw a line ⅜ inch (1 cm) outside your traced lines all

1

2

the way around. Cut out to make your pattern pieces.

Step 2: Place your drawn patterns onto the wrong side of the fabric. Cut A and D from the main fabric and B and C from the contrast fabric.

Step 3: Cut a 16 x 12-inch (40 x 30-cm) piece of the main fabric for the kite back.

Step 4: Cut two strips measuring 2¾ x 44 inches (7 x 112 cm) from the tail fabric.

MAKING THE KITE

Step 1: Place triangles A and B right sides together along the vertical straight edge and stitch together. Repeat with triangles C and D.

Step 2: Place the joined A and B pieces right sides together with the joined C and D pieces and stitch together along the horizontal edge. (Fig. 1)

Step 3: Press your joined kite shape with seams pressed open and then place the interfacing glue-side down on top of the wrong side of the kite and press into place to stiffen your kite.

Step 4: Place the ribbon centrally on top of the vertical seam and topstitch into place.

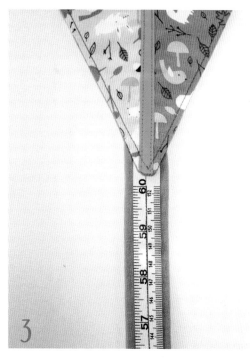

3

4

Repeat to topstitch on top of the horizontal seam. (Fig. 2)

Step 5: Place the kite back fabric right side together with the kite front. Stitch together all the way around the edge, leaving a 2⅜-inch (6-cm) turning gap on one edge.

Step 6: Trim the points and then turn right side out and press the turning gap under. Topstitch all the way around to neaten and close the gap.

Step 7: Cut a 4¾-inch (12-cm) length of ribbon for the hanging loop. Fold it in half and then slip-stitch the ends to the top of the back of the kite.

MAKING THE KITE TAIL

Step 1: Stitch the two fabric strips right sides together along one short end.

Step 2: Fold in half lengthwise, right sides together, and stitch along one short edge and down the length. Turn right side out and then turn the other short edge under by ⅜ inch (1 cm) and slip-stitch closed.

Step 3: Place the tape measure down the center of the tail strip, making sure it's exactly level with one short end. Clip it into place; you won't be able to pin it easily.

Step 4: Topstitch the tape measure into place through the center. Some tape measures are printed with inches on one side and centimeters on the other, so make sure that the side you want is showing on the front.

Step 5: Pin the top end of the tail behind the kite so the 59-inch (150-cm) mark is just below the lower point of the kite and slip-stitch into place, making sure your stitches don't come through to the front. (Fig. 3)

MAKING THE BOWS

Step 1: For each bow (make one for each child), you'll need a 2 x 3⅛-inch (5 x 8-cm) piece of felt. Cut a 1⅝ x 3⅛-inch (4 x 8-cm) piece for the main bow and then cut the corners into neat curves.

Step 2: Cut a ⅜ x 1¼-inch (1 x 3-cm) strip for the knot.

Step 3: Pleat the center of the main bow piece and stitch to hold. Wrap the felt knot strip around the pleated center and oversew neatly to hold the bow in place. (Fig. 4)

Step 4: Glue the back of the knot of each bow to the center of a peg and then clip the peg(s) onto your kite tail to mark the height of your child(ren). For a mark that lasts, draw a line on the tape measure with a pen, too.

PLAY MAT

YOU WILL NEED

- Main fabric: 49 x 44 inch (125 x 112 cm)
- Lining fabric: 43 x 44 inch (110 x 112 cm)
- Trim fabric: 22 x 44 inch (55 x 112 cm)
- Iron-on interfacing: 5½ x 19⅜ inch (14 x 49 cm)
- Cord lock
- Strong nylon cord: ¹⁄₁₆-inch (3-mm) cord
- Snap fastener
- Button
- Matching sewing thread
- Basic sewing kit

Note: Use a ⅜-inch (1-cm) seam allowance throughout.

CUTTING THE FABRIC

Step 1: Stick several sheets of newspaper together to make your paper pattern. Place them on a flat surface, pin a length of string to the center point, and then tie the other end to a pencil. The string needs to reach from the center to just inside the outer edge so that the radius of your circle will be 21¼ inches (54 cm).

Keeping the string taut, draw a circle onto your paper. Cut this out to make your pattern.

Step 2: Cut the main fabric into the following:

Outer play mat: One piece 43 x 43 inches (110 x 110 cm) **Pocket:** Two pieces 6 x 6 inches (15 x 15 cm) each

Step 3: Cut the trim fabric into four strips, 4 x 44 inches (10 x 112 cm) each, for the casing strip and one piece, 5½ x 19⅜ inches (14 x 49 cm), for the carrying strap.

Step 4: Place the main outer fabric and the lining inner fabric squares wrong sides together and then pin the paper pattern on top. Cut around it to make two circles. (Fig. 1)

ATTACHING THE CASING

Step 1: Pin the outer and lining circles wrong sides together and stitch around the edge ¼ inch (5 mm) in to hold them in place.

Step 2: Join the casing strips right sides together at the short ends to make a long strip.

Step 3: Turn one of the short edges over ¾ inch (2 cm) to the wrong side and press.

Step 4: Starting at the turned-over short edge, pin the strip to the lining side of the joined circles right sides together, matching the short edges, and stitch together all the way around.

Step 5: When you have stitched it all the way around and reached the beginning again, trim and turn over the end short edge by ¾ in (2 cm) so the two edges butt up against each other.

Step 6: Turn the other long edge of the strip over by ⅜ inch (1 cm) to the wrong side and pin it

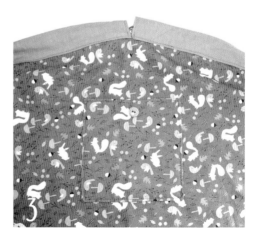

to the outer circle side so that the folded edge meets up with the line of machine stitching. Topstitch in place all the way around through all layers to hold the casing strip in place. (Fig. 2)

MAKING THE POCKET

The pocket is used to store the cord inside when the play mat is closed, and you can also use it to keep any other small items safe.

Step 1: Place the two pieces of pocket fabric right sides together and stitch all the way around, leaving a 1¼-inch (3-cm) turning gap in the center of one side. Turn right side out and press.

Step 2: Pin the pocket to the outer circle, positioning it 4 inches (10 cm) down from the top so that the turned-under edges of the casing strip are centered above it. Topstitch in place down the sides and across the bottom. (Fig. 3)

Step 3: Stitch one half of a snap fastener to the inside of the top of the pocket and the other side of the snap to the outer circle so that they meet to keep the pocket shut.

MAKING THE CARRYING STRAP

Step 1: Press interfacing to the wrong side of the fabric.

Step 2: Fold the strip in half lengthwise right sides together and stitch together across one short end and down the length. Turn right side out, press, and turn the other short end under by ⅜ inch (1 cm).

Step 3: Place the fabric circle outer side up and measure to find the center. Pin one end of your strap at the center and the other directly opposite where the two short ends of the casing strip meet.

Step 4: Stitch the strap securely into place by stitching a square at each end with two diagonal lines through the square to strengthen. (Fig. 4)

FINISHING

Step 1: Thread the cord through the casing and then thread the ends of the cord through the cord lock.

Step 2: To close your play mat, pull up the drawstring cord to collect and hold all your toys safely inside. For safety, tuck the cord into the handy pocket to prevent it from dangling down. You can then carry the playmat or hang it up by the strap.

JIGSAW CUSHIONS

YOU WILL NEED

For one jigsaw cushion:

- Cotton fabric: 20 x 44 inches (51 x 112 cm)
- Lightweight iron-on interfacing:
  14 x 28 inches (35 x 70 cm)
- Polyester fiberfill
- Matching sewing thread
- Basic sewing kit

Note: Use a ¼-inch (5-mm) seam allowance. You will find the template at *www.simplysewingmag.com/101ideas*.

CUTTING THE FABRIC

Step 1: Download, trace, and cut out the jigsaw template. You can use the same template to make all of the cushions; they are double-sided so you can simply flip them over to make them tessellate (fit together) in a different direction.

Step 2: Cut your fabric into the following pieces:

Back and front: two pieces 12 x 12 inches (35 x 35 cm) each.

Sides: two strips 3⅛ x 44 inches (8 x 112 cm) each.

STITCHING THE JIGSAW CUSHIONS

Step 1: Iron interfacing onto the wrong side of both the back and front pieces.

Step 2: Center and pin the jigsaw template on the wrong side of one piece and draw around it. Stay-stitch along the drawn lines.

Step 3: Cut the shape out ⅜ in (1 cm) outside the line all the way around. Clip curves and corners just up to the stay-stitching. Repeat with the other jigsaw piece. (Fig. 1)

Step 4: Place the two side strips right sides together and stitch along one short edge to make one long strip.

Step 5: Turn one short end of the joined side strip under by ¾ inch (2 cm) and then place it right sides together in the center of one of the longer edges of the jigsaw front fabric. Stitch together all the way around.

Step 6: When you get back to where you started, overlap the short ends by ¾ inch (2 cm) and trim to fit. (Fig. 2)

Step 7: Place the jigsaw piece right sides together with the other long edge of the side piece and stitch into place. It's important that the back matches up exactly with the front, so pin it in a few places to make sure the side does not twist. (Fig. 3)

FINISHING

Step 1: Turn your jigsaw piece right side out though the gap and press the seams to make neat edges.

Step 2: Stuff the jigsaw shape firmly through the gap and then slip-stitch the gap closed. (Fig. 4)

Step 3: Make as many jigsaw pieces as you like in the same way, using different fabrics, and then slot them all together to make one big floor cushion.

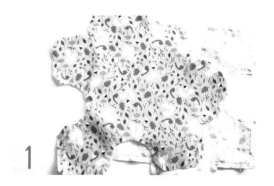

STACKING RINGS

This stacking toy is bursting with interesting colors and textures!

Notes: Use a ³⁄₈-inch (1-cm) seam allowance unless otherwise stated and press all seams open as you go.

You will find the templates needed to make this project at *www.simplysewingmag. com/101ideas* and on page 219.

CUTTING THE FABRIC

Step 1: Trace and cut the pole template from page 219. It is printed in two parts, so simply cut out and join them along the dotted line.

Step 2: The largest ring (Ring E) is printed on the pattern download, and you need to trace all four circles. The bold lines are cutting lines and the dotted lines are stitching lines. For the other four rings, draw the four concentric circles yourself following the diameters given on the table on page 85. We've included measurements for all five rings if you'd rather draw them all yourself.

Step 3: Cut the fabric into the following sizes: **Fabric A:** top and bottom circles, two pieces 5½ x 5½ inches (14 x 14 cm) each; outer gusset, 2³⁄₈ x 13¼ inches (6 x 33½ cm); inner gusset, 2³⁄₈ x 45/8 inches (6 x 11½ cm).

Fabric B: top and bottom circles, two pieces 6½ x 6½ inches (16 x 16 cm) each; outer gusset, 2³⁄₈ x 15¾ inches (6 x 40 cm); inner gusset, 2³⁄₈ x 5¼ inches (6 x 13 cm).

Fabric C: top and bottom circles, two pieces 7½ x 7½ inches (19 x 19 cm) each; outer gusset, 23³⁄₈ x 19³⁄₈ inches (6 x 49 cm); inner gusset, 2³⁄₈ x 5¾ inches (6 x 14½ cm).

YOU WILL NEED

- Cotton fabric A: 10½ x 14 inches (26 x 34 cm)
- Cotton fabric B: 11 x 16 inches (28 x 40 cm)
- Cotton fabric C: 13 x 20 inches (31 x 49 cm)
- Cotton fabric D: 13 x 22 inches (33 x 55cm)
- Cotton fabric E: 21 x 26 inches (52 x 65 cm)
- Lightweight iron-on interfacing: 28 x 35 inches (45 x 90 cm)
- Heavyweight iron-on interfacing: 12 x 5 inches (30 x 12 cm)
- Felt: 6 x 16 inches (15 x 40 cm)
- Polyester fiberfill
- Coordinating ribbons: ³⁄₈-inch (1-cm) width
- Matching sewing thread
- Basic sewing kit

STACKING RINGS CIRCLE DIAMETERS

	INNER CUTTING	INNER STITCHING	OUTER STITCHING	OUTER CUTTING
RING A	⅜-inch (1 cm)	1¼ inches (3 cm)	4 inches (10 cm)	4¾ inches (12 cm)
RING B	½ inch (1½ cm)	1¼ inches (3½ cm)	4¾ inches (12 cm)	5½ inches (14 cm)
RING C	¾ inch (2 cm)	1½ inches (4 cm)	6 inches (15 cm)	6¾ inches (17 cm)
RING D	1 inch (2½ cm)	1¾ inches (4½ cm)	6¾ inches (17 cm)	7½ inches (19 cm)
RING E	1¼ inches (3 cm)	2 inches (5 cm)	8 inches (20 cm)	8¾ inches (22 cm)

Fabric D: top and bottom circles, two pieces 8½ x 8½ inches (21 x 21 cm) each; outer gusset, 2⅜ x 21⅝ inches (6 x 55 cm); inner gusset, 2⅜ x 5½ inches (6 x 14 cm).

Fabric E: top and bottom circles, two pieces 9½ x 9½ inches (24 x 24 cm) each; outer gusset, 2⅜ x 25⅝ inches (6 x 65 cm) inner gusset; 2⅜ x 7⅛ inches (6 x 18 cm); pole, 13¾ x 6 inches (35 x 15 cm).

Step 4: Cut the lightweight interfacing into squares the same size as each of the top and bottom circles for each ring and iron them to the wrong side of each square of fabric.

Step 5: Cut the top and bottom circles for each size of stacking ring in the same way: place the top and bottom pieces of fabric for the circles right sides together and then center and pin the corresponding template on top. Cut around the outer circle and the inner circle, shown by the bold lines, and then transfer the inner and outer stitching lines to each circle—placing the fabric and template against a lightbox or window will help.

DECORATING THE RINGS

You can leave your stacking rings plain or decorate some or all of them. Use the same fabric for the rings and the gussets or alternate them. You need to add the decorations before you assemble the rings.

Ribbon trim: Topstitch a length of ribbon down the center of the length of the outer gusset.

Ribbon loops: Cut a few 2-inch (5-cm) lengths of ribbon to stitch around the ring; how many you use is up to you. Fold one length in half widthwise and then pin the two ends right sides together on top of one of the rings, matching raw edges. Tack into place and then repeat with the other lengths of ribbon so they are spaced evenly. You will stitch these loops securely into place later. (Fig. 1)

Ribbon knots: Cut a few 3-inch (8-cm) lengths of ribbon. For each one, make a knot just above one cut edge and then tack the other end to the outer edge of a ring in the same way as for the ribbon loops.

MAKING THE RINGS

You will make all of the rings in the same way:

Step 1: Take one cut circle of fabric for the ring top and stay-stitch along the inner and outer stitching lines to help stabilize the fabric. Repeat for the circle for the ring bottom.

Step 2: Make small snips, about ⅜ inch (1 cm) apart, from the inner cut-out circle up to the line of stay-stitching, taking care not to cut through the stitches. Repeat for the ring bottom, but this time fold the edges to the wrong side up to the line of stay-stitches and tack. (Fig. 2)

Step 3: Place the two short ends of the inner gusset right sides facing and stitch together. Fold one long edge over by ⅜ inch (1 cm) to the wrong side and tack.

Step 4: Place the untacked edge of the inner gusset tube inside the central hole of the ring top with right sides together. Making small snips in the seam allowance of the tube will help you ease it in. Tack together all the way around.

Step 5: Stitch the tube using small back stitches (it is awkward to stitch by machine). (Fig. 3)

Step 6: Place the two short ends of the outer gusset with right sides facing and stitch together.

Step 7: Pin the outer gusset tube to the outer edge of the ring top and pin together. Stitch together all the way around. (Fig. 4)

Step 8: Join the other side of the outer gusset to the outer edge of the ring bottom.

Step 9: Turn the ring right side out, press, and then stuff through the center hole. Next, slip-stitch the inner ring closed. (Fig. 5)

MAKING THE POLE

Step 1: Pin the pole template to the right side of the pole fabric and cut out around the outer line.

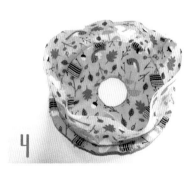

Step 2: Cut (or retrace) your template along the inner line. Pin it to the heavyweight interfacing and cut it out.

Step 3: Press the interfacing to the wrong side of your pole fabric as shown on the template.

Step 4: Fold the top and long sides of the fabric over the interfacing. Turn the bottom edge ⅜ inch (1 cm) to the wrong side.

Step 5: Fold a 4¾-inch (12-cm) length of ribbon in half and then place it on one side of the top, matching raw edges. Topstitch all sides into place. (Fig. 6)

Step 6: Bend the strip together, right side out, and oversew down the length and across the top. (Fig. 7)

Step 7: Stuff your pole to be very firm.

Step 8: Work a running stitch around the bottom, pull to gather, and stitch closed.

Step 9: Cut three circles of felt for the base, each with a 4¾-inch (12-cm) diameter. Pile them up and topstitch around the edge to hold together.

Step 10: Slip-stitch the bottom of the pole to the center of the felt base. (Fig. 8)

5

6

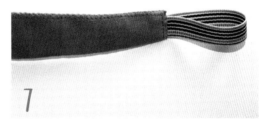

7

8

STOOL COVERS

YOU WILL NEED

- Main fabric: see instructions for details
- Cotton fabric: white, see instructions
- Polyester fiberfill
- Elastic: see instructions for details
- Stool
- Matching sewing thread
- Basic sewing kit

MEASURING AND CUTTING

You can either make a cover to fit over your stool or make a cushion pad to fit on top of the stool and then cover it.

Step 1: Measure the diameter of your stool and under to the legs (including the cushion pad if applicable). The fabric cover needs to fit over the stool and fold underneath.

Step 2: Cut your main fabric into a circle using the diameter you've just measured plus ⅜ inch (1 cm) all the way around.

MAKING THE STOOL COVER

Step 1: Work a machine zigzag stitch all the way around the edge of the fabric to stop it from fraying and then turn it over by ⅜ inch (1 cm) to the wrong side and press. (Fig. 1)

Step 2: Measure around the underside of the stool where the hemmed fabric reaches and cut a piece of elastic to this length plus ¾ inch (2 cm).

Step 3: Fold the fabric in half and then in half again and mark these points with a pin so they are evenly spaced. Fold your elastic in half and then in half again and mark these four points. (Fig. 2)

Step 4: Pin one end of your elastic at the first pin on the fabric so that it is on top of the wrong side of the folded-over edge. Reverse-stitch to secure and then stretch the elastic so that the next pin on the elastic meets with the next pin on the fabric. Machine zigzag-stitch the elastic on top of the folded-over edge. (Fig. 3)

Step 5: When you reach the next pin on the fabric, pull the elastic again to meet it and then continue stitching the elastic into place in the same way. When you reach the end, overlap the elastic on top of the end by ¾ inch (2 cm) and finish securely.

Step 6: Stretch the cover over your stool (and cushion pad, if applicable) so that the elastic tucks underneath to complete.

MAKING THE CUSHION PAD

Step 1: Draw a circle on paper to the same diameter as the top of your stool plus ¾ inch (2 cm). Cut out the circle to make a pattern.

Step 2: Cut two squares of white fabric 2 inches (5 cm) bigger than the paper pattern. Place them right sides together and then draw around the pattern onto the top of one piece of fabric.

Step 3: Stitch the two pieces of fabric together along the drawn line, leaving a turning gap. Trim the seam and turn right side out.

Step 4: Stuff the cushion and then slip-stitch the gap closed. (Fig 4)

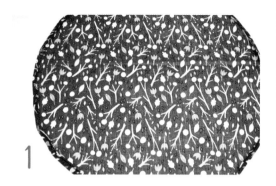

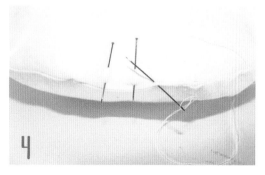

DOWNSTAIRS

Transform your first-floor spaces with a host of handcrafted touches, from delicate table linens to cheery coasters.

KITCHEN BRIGHTS

UPDATE THE HEART OF YOUR HOME

The kitchen is the heart of the home, so treat yours to a fresh look with colorful accessories.

Designer: Rebecca Reid **Styling:** Lisa Jones **Photography:** Philip Sowels

POT HOLDERS

These hanging pot holders will brighten up your cooking space and protect your hands from piping-hot pans when it's time to plate your culinary masterpieces.

DISH TOWELS

Dish towels may be readily available in stores, but there's nothing like stitching your own to brigthen up your kitchen. We've trimmed ours with contrasting fabric and added hanging loops.

DOUBLE OVEN MITT

Take your baked goods out of the oven in style with this pretty and practical double mitt, which has a layer of insulated batting and a contrasting trim.

POCKET-FRONT APRON

Guard your clothes from spills and keep essential utensils handy while you're cooking up a storm with this pocket-front apron. It's made from printed canvas and has webbed straps for maximum durability.

IN THE KITCHEN

TEA COZY

Keep your pot of tea warm with a
bright quilted tea cozy and serve
with fresh scones—the perfect way
to show off your sewing and baking
skills at the same time!

PLASTIC BAG HOLDER

We've all got a hidden-away drawer
overflowing with plastic bags. We
say it's time to reclaim some storage
space by stitching up this pretty
plastic-bag holder.

POT HOLDERS

YOU WILL NEED

- Main fabric: 11½ x 18 inches (29 x 46 cm)
- Contrast fabric: 7 x 18 inches (18 x 46 cm)
- Insulated batting: 16 x 9 inches (41 x 23 cm)
- Basic sewing kit
- Matching sewing thread

MEASUREMENTS

The finished pot holder measures
8 x 8 inches (20 x 20 cm).

Note: Use a ⅝-inch (1½-cm) seam allowance,
unless otherwise stated.

CUTTING

Step 1: From the main fabric, cut the
following::
Front and back: two pieces each, 9 x 9 inches
(23 x 23 cm)

Hanging loop: 6 x 2½ inches (15 x 6 cm).

Step 2: From the contrast fabric, cut the
following:
Pocket front and lining: two pieces each,
7 x 9 inches (18 x 23 cm).

Step 3: From the batting, cut the following:
Pot holder: 9 x 9 inches (23 x 23 cm)
Pocket: 7 x 9 inches (18 x 23 cm)

MAKING THE POCKET

Step 1: Place the two pieces of pocket
fabric right sides together with the pocket
batting on top.

Step 2: Stitch together along the top edge
and then turn the pocket right side out, with
the batting sandwiched in between. Carefully
topstitch along the top edge to neaten and
hold the fabric pieces in place. (Fig. 1)

ADDING THE HANGING LOOP

Step 1: Fold the two long edges of your hanging loop over to the wrong side so they meet in the center.

Step 2: Fold the strip in half lengthwise again and topstitch down to make the loop.

Step 3: Fold the loop in half and pin the two short ends together. Take the front fabric and pin the short ends to one of the top corners, matching raw edges so the loop sits diagonally down from the corner. Tack into place. (Fig. 2)

ASSEMBLING THE POT HOLDER

Step 1: Place all of the pieces on top of each other with raw edges matching in this order: wadding; front, right side up (with the hanging loop attached); pocket, right side down (lined up at the bottom edge); and back.

Step 2: Stitch all of these layers together all the way around, leaving a 2¾-inch (7-cm) gap in the center of the top edge for turning. (Fig. 3)

Step 3: Trim the seams, clip the corners, and then turn right side out through the gap. Press and turn the excess fabric at the gap to the inside.

Step 4: Remove the tacking stitches from the hanging loop so that it lies facing outward. Now topstitch all the way around the edge to hold the fabric layers in place and neaten. (Fig. 4)

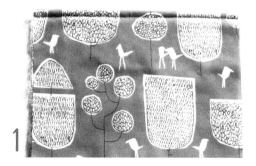

1

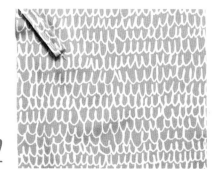

2

3

4

OVEN MITTS

YOU WILL NEED

- Main fabric: 40 x 32 inches (100 x 80 cm)
- Contrast fabric: 9 x 44 inches (22 x 114 cm)
- Insulated batting: 40 x 16 inches (100 x 40 cm)
- Basic sewing kit
- Matching sewing thread

Use insulated batting to protect your hands from high temperatures.

MEASUREMENTS

The finished oven mitts measure 35 x 7 inches (90 x 17 cm).

CUTTING

Step 1: Cut the main fabric into the following:

Main body: 40 x 8 inches (100 x 20 cm)

Lining: 40 x 8 inches (100 x 20 cm)

Mitt front: two pieces, each 10 x 8 inches (25 x 20 cm)

Step 2: Cut the contrast fabric into the following:

Mitt linings: two pieces, each 10 x 8 inches (25 x 20 cm)

Binding: five strips, each 2 x 28 inches (4½ x 70 cm)

CUTTING THE PATTERN PIECES

Step 1: Trace the oven mitt template from the templates on page 217 and cut it out. All seam allowances are included.

Step 2: Place the main body fabric wrong side up. Place the traced mitt pattern centered at the top of the fabric piece and draw around it.

Step 3: Measure 18 inches (46 cm) down from the bottom straight edge of the mitt pattern and place the bottom of the pattern (flipped over) at this point and draw around it. Draw two straight lines joining the bottom edges of the two patterns together as in the diagram on page 103.

Step 4: Cut along your drawn lines to make the oven mitt shape. (Fig. 1)

Place this cut fabric wrong sides together with the lining fabric piece and cut around it. Repeat with the batting.

Step 5: Place the two mitt-front fabric pieces wrong sides together. Center the mitt pattern on top, pin, and then draw around it and cut out both pieces together. One will be the mirror image of the other.

Step 6: Repeat this process for the two mitt-lining pieces and then cut two pieces of batting to the same size.

ASSEMBLING THE MITTS

Step 1: Place one mitt lining right side down with its batting piece on top and then one mitt front right side up on top of the batting.

Step 2: Tack all of the layers together around the edges as well as working vertical and horizontal lines across it spaced 2 inches (5 cm) apart. Now work lines of machine quilting through all three layers. We spaced ours 1¼ inches (3 cm) apart.

Step 3: Take one binding strip and place it right sides together along the straight edge of the mitt. Stitch the binding strip in place through all three layers using a ⅜-inch (1-cm) seam allowance. Trim the binding to meet the mitt edge.

Step 4: Turn the strip over to the back of the mitt and then turn the long edge under by ⅜ inch (1 cm) to match up with the line of stitching. Topstitch into place. (Fig. 2)

Step 5: Repeat to make another mitt.

MAKING THE MITTS

Step 1: Place the main body right side down with the batting on top and then place the lining right side up on top of the batting and tack all layers together.

Step 2: Quilt the three layers together as you did for the mitts. To make sure that the quilting lines on the main body match up with the mitts, space them the same distance apart.

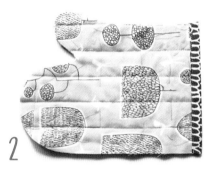

Step 3: Place the quilted main body lining-side up and then place the two quilted mitts right up on either end of it, matching the shaped thumbs and curved ends. Tack together. (Fig. 3)

Step 4: Join the remaining binding strips right sides together at the short ends to make one long strip.

Step 5: Turn one short end of the binding strip over to the wrong side by ⅜ inch (1 cm) and then pin to the edge of the center of the main body with right sides together.

Step 6: Bind all the way around the main body of the glove, encasing the glove as you go in the same way as you did when binding the mitts. (Fig 4)

APRON

YOU WILL NEED

- Main fabric: 51 x 40 inches
  (130 x 100 cm)
- Contrast fabric: 14 x 24 inches
  (35 x 60 cm)
- Webbing: taupe, 1¼ inches x 2¼ yds
  (30 mm x 2 m)
- Two D-rings: silver, 1¼ inches (30 mm)
- Matching sewing thread
- Basic sewing kit

MEASUREMENTS

The finished apron measures 35 x 35 inches
(88 x 88 cm).

Note: Use a ⅝ inch (1½ cm) seam allowance
throughout, unless otherwise stated.

CUTTING

Step 1: Draw half the apron pattern by
following the diagram and using the
measurements on page 103. Seam
allowances are included on the pattern.

Step 2: Fold your main fabric in half lengthwise. Line up the fold line on your pattern with the fold of the fabric, pin, and cut out. Also cut a pocket lining that measures 11 x 23¼ inches (28 x 59 cm).

Step 3: From the contrast fabric, cut the following:

Top edge facing: 2¾ x 11 inches (7 x 28 cm)
Pocket: 11 x 23¼ inches (28 x 59 cm)

ADDING THE FACING AND STRAPS

Step 1: Cut a 3⅝-inch (9 cm) length of webbing for the D-ring loop. Thread it through the D-ring and stitch the short edges together ⅜ inch (1 cm) in from the ends. Matching raw edges, pin it to the right sides of the top of the apron ¾ inch (2 cm) from the right-hand edge.

Step 2: Cut a 24-inch (60-cm) length of webbing for the neck strap and machine zigzag-stitch one end to stop it from fraying. Pin one of the short ends ¾ inch (2 cm) from the left side of the top of the apron, with the right sides together and with the raw edges matching. (Fig. 1)

Step 3: Place the facing right sides together with the top of the apron and pin into place, sandwiching the webbing in between. Stitch together all the way along. (Fig. 2)

Step 4: Turn the facing over to the wrong side. Press and then trim the edges of the facing to match the apron sides. Topstitch along the top to neaten and strengthen the webbing seam. (Fig. 3)

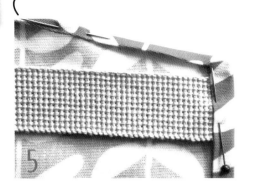

APRON CONTINUED

Step 5: Turn the bottom edge of the facing under by ⅝ inch (1½ cm), pin, and then stitch into place to the main apron fabric. (Fig. 4)

HEMMING THE APRON

Step 1: Turn the curved sides under by ¼ inch (5 mm) and then ¼ inch (5 mm) again and press. Turn the straight sides and the bottom edge under by ⅜ inch (1 cm) and then ⅜ inch (1 cm) again and press.

Step 2: Cut two 25-inch (65-cm) lengths of webbing and machine zigzag-stitch one end of each length to stop them from fraying.

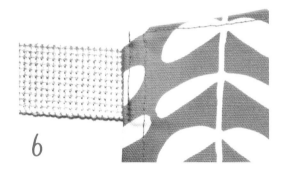

Step 3: Take the unhemmed end of one webbing strap, tuck it inside the turned-under edge of the apron at the top of the straight side, and pin it into place. Repeat with the other strap on the other side of the apron. (Fig. 5)

Step 4: Stitch the turned-under edges to hem, stitching over the straps to secure them.

Step 5: To strengthen the side straps and make them face outward, fold them flat against the wrong side of the apron and topstitch. (Fig. 6)

ADDING A POCKET

Step 1: Place the pocket and pocket lining right sides together and stitch all the way around, leaving a gap along one of the short edges for turning.

Step 2: Turn the pocket right side out and turn the excess fabric at the gap to the inside and press. Topstitch two rows along the top edge of the pocket to neaten and decorate. (Fig. 7)

Step 3: Pin the pocket to the front of your apron following the pocket-positioning guide on the diagram. Stitch in place down the sides and across the bottom edge.

Step 4: To divide the pocket into sections, stitch a vertical line down the center of the pocket and then stitch another line parallel to this line ¼ inch (5 mm) away. Stitch another pair of vertical lines through the center of the left pocket as shown on the diagram. (Fig. 8)

PATTERN DIAGRAM

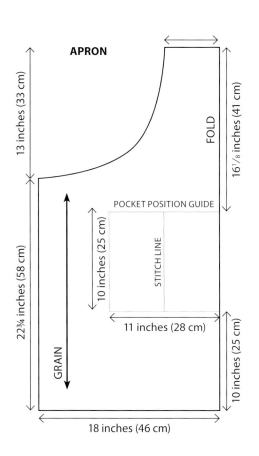

APRON

13 inches (33 cm)

16¹⁄₈ inches (41 cm)

FOLD

POCKET POSITION GUIDE

10 inches (25 cm)

STITCH LINE

11 inches (28 cm)

22¾ inches (58 cm)

GRAIN

10 inches (25 cm)

18 inches (46 cm)

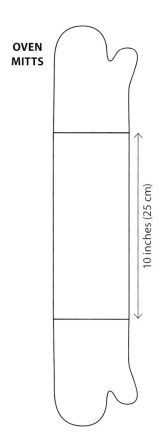

OVEN MITTS

10 inches (25 cm)

PLASTIC-BAG HOLDER

YOU WILL NEED

- Top fabric: 9½ x 17 inches (24 x 43 cm)
- Center and loop fabric: 6 x 17 inches (16 x 43 cm)
- Bottom fabric: 9½ x 17 inches (24 x 43 cm)
- Elastic: ⅜ x 18 inches (1 x 45 cm)
- Matching sewing thread

MEASUREMENTS

The finished plastic-bag holder measures 18 x 8 inches (45 x 20 cm).

Note: Use a ⅝-inch (1½-cm) seam allowance.

JOINING THE FABRICS

Step 1: Cut the center fabric into two pieces, each measuring 3 x 17 inches (8 x 43 cm) for the center strip and hanging loop.

Step 2: Place the top fabric strip right sides together with the center fabric strip and sew along the long edge. Press the seam open.

Step 3: Place the bottom fabric right sides together along the lower edge of the center strip and stitch together. Press the seam open.

Step 4: Fold the joined fabric pieces in half lengthwise, right sides together, and pin, matching the seams carefully. Stitch together all the way down the length. (Fig. 1)

MAKING A HANGING LOOP

Step 1: Fold the two long edges of the hanging loop over to the wrong side so they meet in the center.

Step 2: Fold the strip in half lengthwise again and topstitch down to make the hanging loop.

FINISHING THE ENDS

Step 1: Turn the top edge over by ⅜ inch (1 cm) and then by ⅝ inch (1½ cm) to the wrong side and press.

Step 2: Making sure the stitched bag seam is in the center of one side, slip one of the raw ends of the hanging loop under the turned-under edge and pin in place. (Fig. 2)

Step 3: Place the other raw end of the hanging loop under the turned-under edges directly opposite the first end and pin into place.

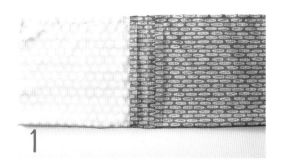

Step 4: Stitch the turned-over top edge all the way around, close to the edge, encasing the hanging loop ends as you go. Leave a ¾-inch (2-cm) gap for threading the elastic through later.

Step 5: To make the hanging loop hang upward, fold it up above the bag and topstitch just along the top edge of the casing and loop at both ends of the loop. (Fig. 3)

Step 6: Make a casing at the bottom end of the bag in the same way.

ADDING THE ELASTIC

Step 1: Cut the elastic into two pieces: 12 inches (30 cm) for the top and 6 inches (15 cm) for the bottom. The elastic at the top is longer so you can easily fill the bag holder with plastic bags, and the bottom end is shorter so that the plastic bags don't fall out and you can pull out one at a time.

Step 2: Thread the longer length of elastic through the top of the bag holder and then knot the ends and push them into the casing. Slip-stitch the gap closed. Repeat at the bottom end of the bag with the shorter length of elastic. (Fig. 4)

TEA COZY

To simplify the process, use ready-made bias binding to finish the edges of your cozy.

YOU WILL NEED

- Main fabric: 9 x 28 inches (23 x 70 cm)
- Contrast fabric: 16 x 28 inches (40 x 70 cm)
- Binding fabric: 63 x 2⅜ inches (160 x 6 cm)
- Insulated batting: 12 x 28 inches (30 x 70 cm)
- Matching sewing thread

Note: Use a ⅝-inch (1½-cm) seam allowance. The tea cozy pattern is on page 216.

CUTTING

Step 1: From the main fabric, cut two pieces for the front and back, 9⅛ x 13¾ inches (23 x 35 cm) each.

Step 2: From the contrast fabric, cut the following: Front and back: two strips, 3⅛ x 13¾ inches (8 x 35 cm) each.

Lining: two pieces, 12 x 13¾ inches (30 x 35 cm) each.

Step 3: From the binding fabric, cut the following:

Lower-edge binding: two strips, 2⅜ x 13 inches (6 x 33 cm) each.

Curved-edge binding: 2⅜ x 32 inches (6 x 80 cm)

Hanging loop: 2⅜ x 5 inches (6 x 12 cm).

Step 4: From the batting, cut two pieces, 12 x 13¾ inches (30 x 35 cm) each.

MAKING THE PIECES

Step 1: Trace the tea cozy template from page 216 and cut it out.

Step 2: Place one main fabric piece and one contrast strip right sides together and stitch along the lower shorter edge of the main fabric. Turn right side out and press. Repeat with the other pieces of main and contrast fabric.

Step 3: Place the tea cozy pattern over one joined fabric piece and cut it out. Repeat for the other joined fabrics to make the tea cozy front and back. (Fig. 1)

Step 4: From the contrast fabric lining and batting, cut two pattern pieces of each.

ASSEMBLING THE FABRIC LAYERS

Step 1: Lay one lining piece right side down with a piece of batting on top and then the joined tea cozy front, right side up, on top of that.

Step 2: Tack all of the layers together around the edges and work vertical and horizontal lines across, spaced 2 inches (5 cm) apart. Now work horizontal lines of machine quilting through all layers. We spaced ours 1¼ inches (3 cm) apart. (Fig. 2)

Step 3: Take one lower edge binding and place it right sides together, matching raw edges along the lower edge of the quilted tea cozy front. Stitch in place. Turn the strip over to the back of the tea cozy front and then turn the long edge under by ⅝ inch (1½ cm) to match up with the line of stitching. Topstitch in place.

Step 3: Repeat the steps to make the tea cozy back.

MAKING THE HANGING LOOP

Step 1: Fold the two long edges of the hanging loop strip over to the wrong side so they meet in the center.

Step 2: Fold the strip in half lengthwise again and topstitch down to make the hanging loop.

BINDING THE COZY

Step 1: Place the tea cozy front and back together with linings facing and then tack all six layers together around the curved edge.

Step 2: Turn one short end under on the curved-edge binding strip and then place it right sides together along the bottom of the curved edge. Stitch the binding strip in place through all of the tea cozy layers. When you reach the end, turn the short end under to match the bottom of the cozy and trim. (Fig. 3)

Step 3: Turn the strip over to the back of the tea cozy and then turn the long edge under by ⅝ inch (1½ cm) to match up with the line of stitching.

Step 4: Fold the loop in half and pin the raw ends at the center top of the tea cozy, tucking them under the turned-under binding. Fold the loop upward and then slip-stitch into place. (Fig. 4)

Step 5: Slip-stitch or machine-topstitch the binding in place, encasing the loop as you go. Remove all of the tacking stitches to finish.

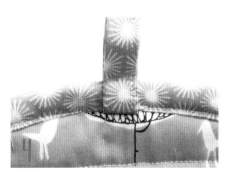

DISH TOWEL

Wash your dish towel before use to remove fabric finishes and make it more absorbent.

YOU WILL NEED

- Main fabric: 25 x 22 inches (63 x 56 cm)
- Contrast fabric: 9 x 22 inches (23 x 56 cm)
- Basic sewing kit
- Matching sewing thread

MEASUREMENTS

The finished dish towel measures 28 x 20 inches (70 x 50 cm).

CUTTING

Step 1: From the contrast fabric, cut the following:

Border: 6¾ x 22 inches (17 x 56 cm).
Hanging loop: 2¼ x 22 inches (6 x 20 cm).

JOINING THE FABRICS

Because you'll see both sides of your dish towel, it will look better if you finish the border and main fabric seam neatly. This is optional, but it will look professional. A flat felled seam works well because it will look neat from both sides.

Step 1: Place the main fabric and contrast border strip right sides together. Stitch together using a ¾-inch (2-cm) seam allowance along the lower short edge of the main fabric and top long edge of the border fabric.

Step 2: Trim ⅜ inch (1 cm) off the main fabric seam allowance so that it's half the width of the border fabric seam allowance. (Fig. 1)

Step 3: Fold the border fabric seam allowance over so it lies on top of the main fabric seam allowance and press. (Fig. 2)

Step 4: Fold the border fabric seam allowance under and press so it wraps around the main fabric seam allowance and the raw edges are tucked inside. (Fig. 3)

Step 5: Stitch this folded-over seam allowance in place close to the edge. (Fig. 4)

MAKING A HANGING LOOP

Step 1: Fold the two long edges of the loop fabric strip over to the wrong side to meet in the center.

Step 2: Fold the strip in half lengthwise again and topstitch down to make the loop strip.

HEMMING THE DISH TOWEL

Step 1: Turn all four edges of the joined dish towel over by ⅝ inch (1½ cm) to the wrong side and then by ⅝ inch (1½ cm) again and press.

Step 2: Fold the hanging loop in half and slip the raw ends under the turned-over hem in the top left corner and pin.

Step 3: Stitch the hem all the way down, close to the edge, stitching through the hanging loop as you go.

Step 4: Turn the loop over so it sticks out beyond the edge of the dish towel and stitch it down to lie flat.

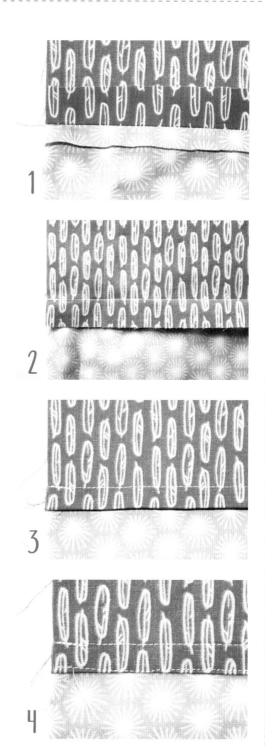

CREATIVE COASTERS

FUN WITH FELT WEAVING

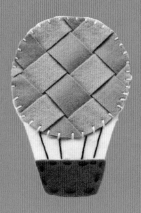

Combine weaving and hand sewing to make Diana Stainton's cute hot-air balloon coasters.

Diana is the creator of Pygmy Cloud (www.pygmycloud.com), a little brand of playful and quirky plush toys and housewares.

COASTERS

YOU WILL NEED

- Small quantities of felt in teal, gray, white, and brown
- Embroidery floss, brown and white
- Embroidery needle
- Fabric glue
- Thin cardboard
- Erasable pen or pencil
- Scissors

Step 1: Trace the template from page 218 onto thin cardboard, cut it out, and trace around it onto the white felt using the erasable pen or pencil. (Fig. 1)

Step 2: Cut out the hot-air balloon shape. This will be the base of the design. (Fig. 2)

Step 3: Cut four strips of teal felt and four strips of gray felt, each measuring ¾ x 4 inches (2 x 10 cm). (Fig. 3)

Step 4: Place the gray strips vertically and start to weave the teal strips horizontally. (Fig. 4)

Step 5: Weave all of the strips together to look like this. (Fig. 5)

Step 6: Dab fabric glue sparingly onto the white felt in the top circle area only. (Fig. 6)

Step 7: Place the woven felt piece on the white felt circle area so the strips sit at an angle. Press down firmly and allow to dry. (Fig. 7)

Step 8: Trim the woven felt piece into a circle shape, using the white felt base as a guide. (Fig. 8)

Step 9: Cut the brown felt into a basket shape to match the white felt base. Using brown thread, sew the basket onto the white felt with a running stitch. (Fig. 9)

Step 10: With brown thread, sew four long stitches for ropes between the balloon and basket. (Fig. 10)

Step 11: Using white thread, sew around the edge of the balloon circle using a blanket stitch to finish. Time for tea! (Fig. 11)

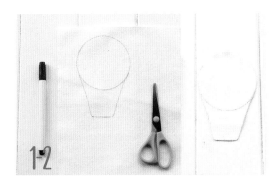

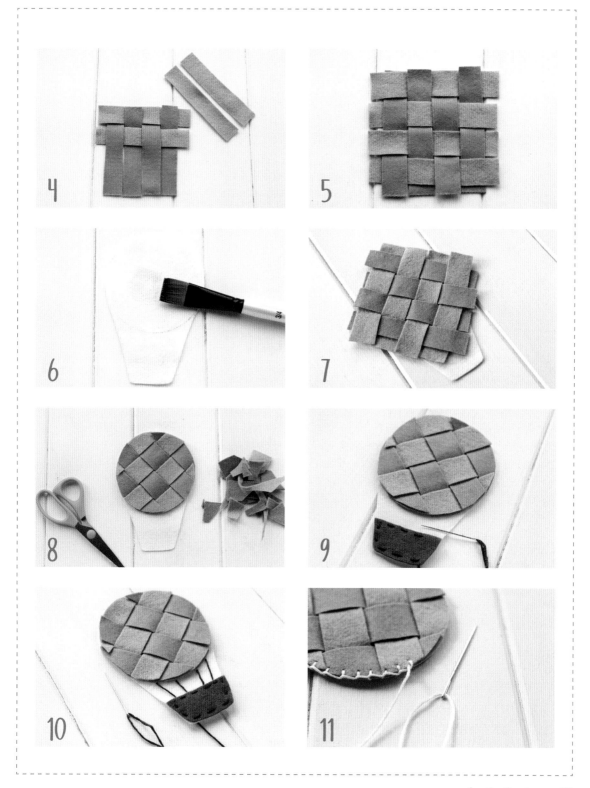

THE PERFECT SETTING

CREATE BEAUTIFUL TABLE LINENS

Classy table linens add to any
occasion, but don't worry if it's
not in your budget to buy some—
it's so easy to make your own!

Designer: Rebecca Reid **Styling:** Lisa Jones **Photography:** Philip Sowels

YOUR CHOICE OF NAPKIN

We mixed up the styles and finishes of the napkins on our table setting, and you can do the same. We've covered three key techniques in our instructions: hemstitch, curved corners, and fraying. You'll also learn how to make the perfect mitered corner.

DINING STYLE

COVER UP AND LEARN NEW SKILLS

If your kitchen chairs look shabby, this project is perfect. You can even add a small cushion under the chair cover if your chair doesn't have any padding. You'll also learn new skills, such as making a toile (see page 128), that will come in handy for future sewing assignments.

PATCH POCKET PLACE MAT

Keep your knife, fork, and spoon neatly in place with this inspired table-setting design. Choose different finishing techniques to make yours unique; we've frayed the edges of both the mat and the pocket.

ZIGZAG NAPKIN

YOU WILL NEED

- Checkered fabric, 17¾ x 17¾ inches (45 x 45 cm)
- Light gray linen fabric, 17¾ x 17¾ inches (45 x 45 cm).
- Matching sewing thread

MEASUREMENTS

The finished napkin measures 17¾ x 17¾ inches (45 x 45 cm).

MAKING EACH NAPKIN

Step 1: Take your square of checkered fabric and draw a curve on each of the four corners by tracing around the edge of a glass or similar round object. (Fig. 1)

Step 2: Cut out the curves carefully along the drawn lines to give you neat, soft corners. (Fig. 2)

Step 3: Using your sewing machine, work a narrow zigzag stitch all around the edge of your fabric. Move the fabric slowly as you go around each curved corner to keep the stitches right at the edge. Use a thread color that blends in with your fabric. (Fig. 3)

Step 4: Repeat Steps 1–3 with your square of linen fabric. This time, use a thread color that contrasts with your fabric. (Fig. 4)

Step 5: Finish by trimming off any loose thread ends and pressing for a crisp finish.

FRAYED NAPKIN

YOU WILL NEED

- Dark gray linen fabric, 17¾ x 17¾ inches (45 x 45 cm)
- Matching sewing thread

MEASUREMENTS

The finished napkin measures 17¾ x 17¾ inches (45 x 45 cm).

MAKING EACH NAPKIN

Step 1: Take your square of fabric and work a line of straight machine stitches all the way around, ⅝ inch (1½ cm) in from the raw edge. (Fig. 1)

Step 2: Carefully remove the linen threads outside your line of stitching on all sides. (Fig. 2)

Step 3: If you'd like to add an extra decorative touch to your napkin, as we have, remove some horizontal threads across one edge of the napkin; we positioned ours 1½, 2½, and 3¼ inches (4, 6, and 8 cm) up from the lower edge. Next, work a very narrow zigzag stitch along the position of the drawn thread, using the space left by the thread as a guide to keeping your stitches straight. (Fig. 3)

Step 4: Stitch over the remaining two drawn thread lines in the same way. (Fig. 4)

Step 5: Finish by trimming off any loose thread ends and pressing for a crisp finish.

HEMSTITCH NAPKIN

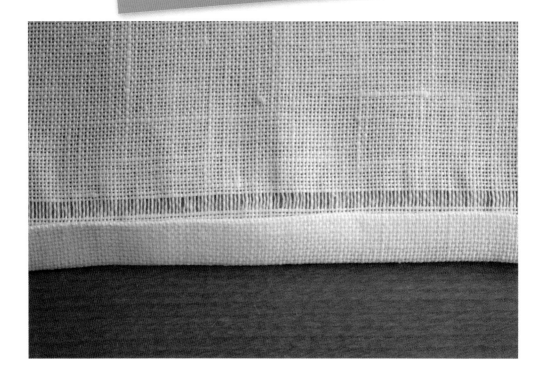

YOU WILL NEED

- Off-white linen fabric, 20 x 20 inches (51 x 51 cm)
- Embroidery floss

MEASUREMENTS

The finished napkin measures 17¾ x 17¾ inches (45 x 45 cm).

DRAWING OUT THREADS AND MITERING THE CORNERS

Step 1: Take your square of fabric and follow the instructions on page 122 to draw out threads and make a mitered corner.

WORKING A HEMSTITCH EDGE

Step 1: To work the hemstitches, use two strands of embroidery floss in a color that matches your linen fabric. We used a contrasting color thread in these photos so you can see it more clearly.

Anchor your thread in one corner of the linen, at the outer point of the mitered corner, and work some tiny slip stitches to hold the mitered corner in place.

Working from right to left and holding the linen with the hem facing away from you, push the needle under four or five of the drawn threads. (Fig. 1)

Step 2: Pull the needle and thread through the fabric and give it a little tug toward the right to pull the drawn threads together. (Fig. 2)

Step 3: Push the needle back into the fabric at the same point as in Step 1 and then bring the needle out of the fabric at the same point as in Step 2 to take your thread back around the same group of drawn threads. Next, insert your needle under a few threads at the edge of the hem. (Fig. 3)

Pull the needle all the way through the hem to secure the group of drawn threads and to stitch down the hem.

Step 4: Repeat the process from Step 1 to work hemstitches all along the first edge of your napkin. (Fig. 4)

When you reach the next corner, slip-stitch the mitered corner together, as you did previously, and then continue to work hemstitches along the next edge. Continue all around the napkin edge. When you reach the first corner again, fasten off the thread.

Step 5: Finish by trimming off any loose thread ends and pressing for a crisp finish.

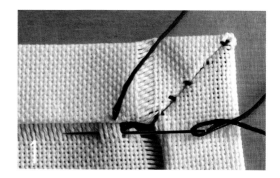

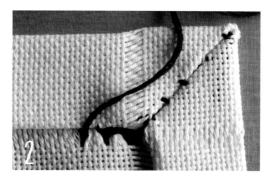

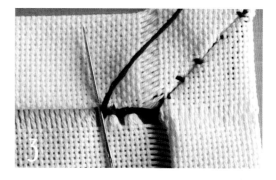

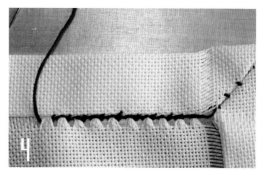

HOW TO DRAW THREADS AND MITER THE CORNERS

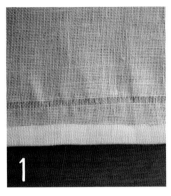
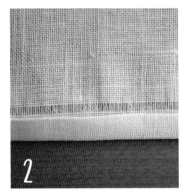
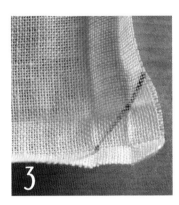
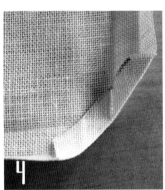

1. Measure 1¼ inches (3 cm) in from one edge of the fabric and pull out a thread of the linen. Next, pull out three more threads, working inward. (Fig. 1)
2. Fold over the edge by ⅝ inch (1½ cm). Repeat on all four sides of the linen square and press. (Fig. 2)
3. Miter the corners as follows: Open out the folds and, at one corner, draw a line across the first set of folds, using Fig. 3 as a guide.
4. Cut along this drawn line to trim off the excess corner fabric. Fold this new edge inward diagonally at the inner corner fold, using Fig. 4 as a guide.
5. Refold all four sides of the linen, following the fold lines you made previously. Press your mitered corner and pin into place. The corner should now come together neatly into a point. (Fig. 5)
6. Now you can work hemstitches through the drawn threads all around your napkin, following the instructions on pages 120-1. (Fig. 6)

BASKET LINER

Serve bread in style with this beautifully lined basket!

YOU WILL NEED

- Checkered fabric, see instructions for sizing
- Twill tape to fit around the basket
- Matching sewing thread

MEASUREMENTS

The finished liner will fit your basket.

Note: These basic instructions are for a basket with straight sides. If your basket has slanted sides, like ours, then all you need to do is cut the top edge of each side to the top edge basket measurement (including seam and ease allowances). Your side pieces will have angled side edges so that your liner fits snugly. Make sure you leave the bottom and top seam and casing allowances straight, though, so that the pieces sew together neatly.

CUTTING

Step 1: Measure inside the base of your basket and add 1 inch (2½ cm) for ease and seam allowance all around. These are the measurements for your base piece.

Step 2: Measure the two short sides and two long sides of your basket. For the height of each side piece, the measurement should start at the base and then fold over the basket by 1½ inches (4 cm); you also need to add 1 inch (2½ cm) for ease and seam allowances, plus an extra 1½ inches (4 cm) for the casing at the top edge. For the width of each side piece, use the same measurements as the corresponding side of the base piece.

Step 3: Use the measurements you've taken to cut out one base piece, two short side pieces, and two long side pieces from your checkered fabric. (Fig. 1)

ASSEMBLING THE LINER

Step 1: Join the four side pieces together, alternating long and short sides, to make one continuous side piece. (Fig. 2)

Step 2: Join the base piece to the base of the continuous side piece, making sure that you place right sides together and pivot at each corner.

Step 3: Fold the top edge of the liner to the wrong side by ⅝ inch (1½ cm) and then by 1 inch (2½ cm) to form the casing. Stitch this in place, close to the edge of the casing. (Fig. 3)

Step 4: Snip away the stitches in one of the side seams of the casing and thread the twill tape through the casing. Place the liner inside the basket and then finish by pulling the tape to tighten and tying the ends in a bow. (Fig. 4)

PLACE MAT

Use a contrasting fabric on the pocket to show off the details and complement other linens on your table.

YOU WILL NEED

- Checkered fabric, 2 pieces
  12 x 15¾ inches (30 x 40 cm)
- Striped fabric, 6 x 4 inches (15 x 10 cm)
- Matching sewing thread

MEASUREMENTS

The finished place mat measures
2 x 15 ¾ inches (30 x 40 cm).

MAKING YOUR MAT

Step 1: Cut your three fabric pieces to the measurements given at left. (Fig. 1)

Step 2: Pin the two large checkered pieces together, with wrong sides together, and then use your sewing machine to work a zigzag stitch all the way around all four sides, ⅕ inch (½ cm) in from the raw edge. (Fig. 2)

Step 3: To fray the edges, carefully remove the fabric threads outside the line of zigzag stitches. (Fig. 3)

Step 4: Work a line of zigzag stitches across one short edge of the striped pocket fabric, ⅕ inch (½ cm) from the edge, starting and

PLACE MAT CONTINUED

finishing ⅕ inch (½ cm) in from each end. Fray the fabric edge as in Step 3. (Fig. 4)

Step 5: Pin the pocket to the place mat, positioning it 1 inch (2½ cm) up from the bottom edge and 1 inch (2½ cm) in from the right-hand side. Zigzag-stitch the pocket into place down one side, along the bottom, and up the other side, ⅕ inch (½ cm) in from the raw edges. (Fig. 5)

Step 6: Fray the side and bottom edges of the pocket and then trim off any loose thread ends and press for a crisp finish.(Fig. 6)

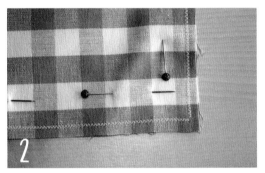

CHAIR COVER

YOU WILL NEED

- Large checkered fabric for seat cover, see pattern and cutting notes for sizing
- Small checkered fabric for binding and buttons, see instructions for sizing
- Cotton lining fabric, see instructions for sizing
- Velcro sew-on hook and loop, 8 inches (20 cm)
- Six self-cover buttons, ¾ inch (19 mm)
- Matching sewing thread

MEASUREMENTS

The finished cover will fit your chair.

MAKING A PATTERN

Step 1: Make a pattern for your chair cover. Place a sheet of paper on your chair seat and draw around its outer edges. Add 4¾ inches (12 cm) to all four sides for the chair cover's skirt. At the back corners of the cover, add ⁴⁄₅ inch (2 cm) at the back and 1½ inches (4 cm) at the side to give you extra fabric to wrap around the legs. You will also need to cut a rounded opening in the back corners so they

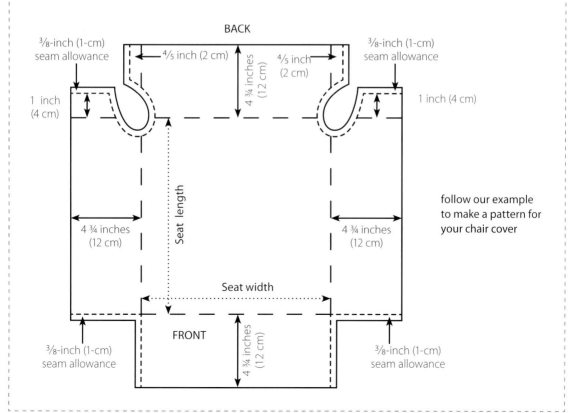

follow our example to make a pattern for your chair cover

fit around the legs of your chair. See the diagram on page 127, and there's a full-size example at *www.simplysewingmag.com/101ideas*.

Step 2: After drawing the pattern, add the ⅜-inch (1-cm) seam allowances to the front square corners and the back rounded corners; you will bind the other edges of the cover later.

MAKING A TOILE

A toile is a test piece made in fabric to get the pattern and fitting correct; you can use any spare fabric for this. Cutting out the chair cover is straightforward if you follow the pattern, but getting the curves just right so they fit around your chair is easier if you make a toile. Place the fabric over your chair and cut around the legs to get the perfect curves. If your chair is not exactly square but wider at the front, you can adjust the pattern's fit using this method. It saves time in the long run if you get the pattern right at the start!

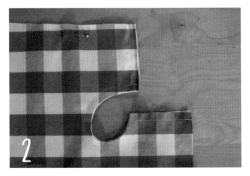

CUTTING

Cut out your main fabric, using the pattern, and then cut out an identical piece from the cotton lining fabric.

MAKING THE CORNERS

Note: Use a ⅜-inch (1-cm) seam allowance throughout.

Step 1: To make the front seat corners, place the two corner edges right sides together and stitch to make a neat right angle. Repeat this with the two front corners on the lining fabric. (Fig. 1)

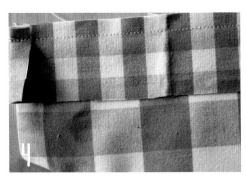

Step 2: Place your main fabric and lining wrong sides together and pin together around the back curved edges. Stitch together around both sides of the curved and short edges. Repeat for the other back curved edge. (Fig. 2)

Step 3: Clip the seams and then turn your seat cover right side out and press. (Fig. 3)

MAKING THE COVER

Step 1: Bind the back edge and the front and side edges. Cut the small checkered fabric into 1½-inch (4-cm) strips, one to fit across the back and one to fit around the sides and back. Place the strip right sides together on top of the right side of the seat cover and lining, turning the short ends over, and then stitch into place. (Fig. 4)

Step 2: Turn the other long edge over ⅝ inch (1 cm) to the wrong side. (Fig. 5)

Step 3: Fold the binding around the seat cover and lining, stitch into place, and then topstitch around the curved corner to neaten. (Fig. 6)

ADDING VELCRO AND BUTTONS

Step 1: Sew Velcro to the side edges of the back corners. The hook part of the Velcro goes on the right side of the side of the cover, and the loop section goes on the wrong side of the back of the cover. You can machine-stitch the hook section in place, but it's best to hand-sew the loop section to just the lining so the stitches can't be seen from the front. (Fig. 7)

Step 2: For decoration, cover six buttons following the package's instructions. Stitch them in place down the back edges of the cover and then slip the cover over your chair and Velcro it in place. (Fig. 8)

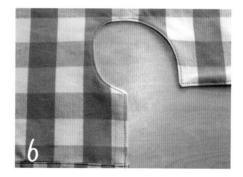

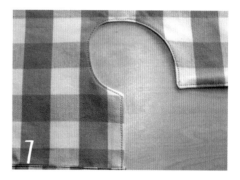

TABLE RUNNER

Work slowly and carefully through each step for making mitered corners—the results are worth it!

YOU WILL NEED

- Striped fabric, see instructions for sizing
- Matching sewing thread

MEASUREMENTS

The finished table runner measures 15¾ inches (40 cm) wide.

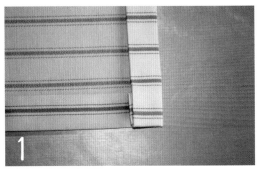

CUTTING

Step 1: Cut your fabric 19¾ inches (50 cm) wide and the length to fit your table plus 2 inches (5 cm) at each end for seam allowances.

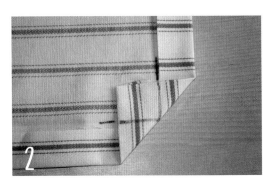

HOW TO MITER A CORNER

Step 1: Fold the fabric over by 1 inch (2½ cm) all the way around, press, and then fold it over again by 1 inch (2½ cm) and press. (Fig. 1)

Step 2: Keeping your runner wrong side up, unfold the second fold you pressed and then fold the corner inward so that the pressed creases line up with the creases from the second fold. These are marked in purple in the photo so you can see them. (Fig. 2)

Step 3: Press this fold to get a crease and then unfold it. (Fig. 3)

Step 4: Fold the corner so the runner is right sides together, making sure to line up the outer folded edges. The last crease you made should line up through the layers. Pin and then stitch along this line, which is marked in purple on the photo. Trim the seam. (Fig. 4)

Step 5: Turn the mitered corner right side out and press. (Fig. 5)

FINISHING YOUR RUNNER

Step 1: Miter the other three corners in the same way.

Step 2: Topstitch the folded-over edges down, keeping the needle in the fabric as you turn each corner for a neat finish. (Fig. 6)

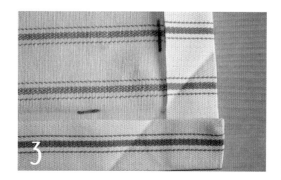

DECOR FOR DOORS

SHOW YOUR DOORS SOME LOVE!

Give your doors some fabric love with this muffler, doorstop, and draft stopper set by Dawn Worthington.

Polka dots are always in fashion

We love the stylish look of traditional homes—their period features add character and detail—but they can be drafty. Here, we look at the traditional ways of solving this problem with a set of simple door accessories—a door muffler, doorstop, and draft stopper—so you don't have to turn up the heat to stay warm. These accessories make such a difference, even on spring and summer evenings.

This project is perfect for using up leftover fabric (you can use different fabric on each side of your draft stopper if you have only small amounts). We've also discovered some clever ways of using materials that most people have around the house so you can save some money if you prefer to upcycle. For example, we've used elastic hair bands to keep the door muffler in place, and bags of rice or worn-out socks and tights for stuffing the doorstop and draft stopper. But if you prefer to eat your rice (and make sure you don't get any unwanted visitors), we recommend using pebbles and batting or plastic pellets (such as beanbag filler).

You can also personalize your draft stopper by adding lavender or your favorite essential oil to the stuffing to give it a sweet scent. Dawn's design allows you to easily remove the insert to wash the cover or even replace it if you need to. One of her helpful tips is to attach the draft stopper to the bottom of your door with a strip of Velcro to keep it firmly in place when you open and close the door, so you don't have to reposition it every time. We think that's genius!

DOOR MUFFLER

DOORSTOP

DRAFT STOPPER

DOOR MUFFLER

YOU WILL NEED

- Basic sewing kit
- Matching sewing thread
- Sewing machine
- Cotton fabric, 8 x 8 inches (20 x 20 cm)
- Quilt batting, 4 x 8 inches (10 x 20 cm)
- Elastic hair ties or other elastic bands

MEASUREMENTS

The completed door muffler measures
6¾ x 2¾ inches (17 x 7 cm).

Note: Seam allowance is ⅝ inch (1½ cm), unless
otherwise stated.

MAKING THE DOOR MUFFLER

Step 1: Before cutting, check that the 4 x 8-inch
(10 x 20-cm) size will reach around your door to each

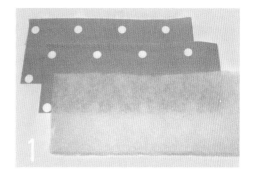

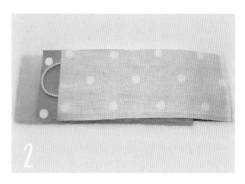

handle; adapt if needed. Next, cut your cotton fabric in half to give you two pieces measuring 4 x 8 inches (10 x 20 cm). (Fig. 1)

Step 2: Place the two fabric pieces together with right sides facing, then add the wadding piece underneath. Place the hairbands or looped lengths of elastic in between the two fabric pieces, as shown. (Fig. 2)

Pin together securely. If you're using elastic loops, place the join on the outside of the fabric layers, close to the raw edge of the fabric. Make sure the bulk of the hairband or elastic is inside the fabric layers (this is the part that will be on the outside of the finished muffler). (Fig. 3)

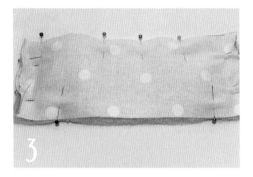

Step 3: Using your sewing machine, stitch the three pieces together around the outside, ensuring that the hairbands or elastic loops are sewn firmly in place. Make sure you leave a small opening (approximately 2 inches [5cm]) along one of the longer edges—this is to turn your fabric through. (Fig. 4)

Step 4: Trim the wadding close to the stitching and then clip the corners of all layers to reduce bulk. (Fig. 5)

Step 5: Turn the muffler right side out through the gap and then use a round-ended object to push the corners out (we used the end of a makeup brush).

Step 6 Topstitch around the muffler as close to the edge as you can. When you reach the gap, tuck the fabric inside and continue topstitching—this will close the opening. (Fig. 6)

Hang an end over each side of your door handle and enjoy the silence when the door closes.

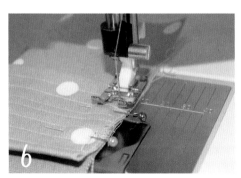

DOORSTOP

Weight your doorstop with any inexpensive bag of rice.

YOU WILL NEED

- Basic sewing kit
- Matching sewing thread
- Sewing machine
- Cotton fabric, 17¾ x 17¾ inches (45 x 45 cm)
- Weighted filling (such as rice or plastic pellets)
- Funnel (optional)

MEASUREMENTS

The finished doorstop measures 4¾ x 4¾ inches (12 x 12 cm).

Note: Seam allowance is ⅝ inch (1½ cm), unless otherwise stated.

MAKING THE DOORSTOP

Step 1: Measure and cut six squares of cotton fabric, each measuring 6 x 6 inches (15 x 15 cm), for the sides of your cube. Cut one piece of fabric to 8 x 6 inches (20 x 15 cm); this will be the handle of your doorstop.

Step 2: With right sides together, fold your 8 x 6-inch (20 x 15-cm) handle piece in half along the longest length. Pin and sew together, leaving the short ends open. Turn this piece right side out and position the seam at

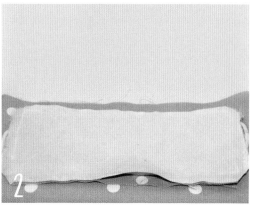

the center back. Press flat, making sure the seam allowance is also flat. Topstitch several times along the length to give the handle extra strength.

Step 3: Place right sides together and then pin and sew four of your squares together to form an open-ended "cube" shape. (Fig. 1)

Step 4: Clip the seam corners to reduce bulk and then press the seam allowances open.

Step 5: Place your handle piece on top of one of the remaining squares, with the center back face down. Line up the handle piece so it runs along the center of the square. (Fig. 2)

Pin and then sew both ends of the handle in place, ⅜ inch (1 cm) from the raw edge of the fabric. (Fig. 3)

Step 6: Pin the two remaining squares to the previously stitched pieces to form the top and bottom of your cube. (Fig. 4)

Stitch all around the top square (including the handle), ⅝ inch (1½ cm) from the raw fabric edge. We recommend stitching slowly when you reach the corners. Stitch around the bottom square, but make sure you leave a small opening (approximately 2 inches [5 cm]) for the filling.

Step 7: Turn the cube right side out through the opening. Use a round-ended object to push the corners out neatly (we used the end of a makeup brush). (Fig. 5)

Step 8: To make it easier to clear up any spillage, place the cube in a container. Using a funnel for ease, fill your cube with the weighted filler. (Fig. 6) Once the cube is full, hand-sew the opening closed using slip stitches.

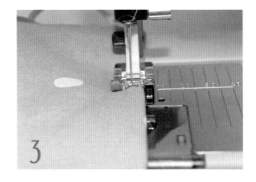

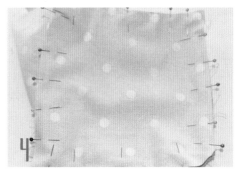

DRAFT STOPPER

A draft stopper is easy to make with a few basic items.

YOU WILL NEED

- Basic sewing kit
- Matching sewing thread
- Sewing machine
- Cotton fabric, 15¾ x 39½ inches (40 x 100 cm)
- Two buttons
- Excluder insert (see Step 9)

MEASUREMENTS

The finished draft stopper (for a door width of approximately 31½ inches [80 cm]) measures 32 x 6¾ inches (81½ x 17 cm).

Note: Seam allowance is ⅝ inch (1½ cm), unless otherwise stated..

The fabric amounts given are for making a draft stopper for a door width of approximately inches 31½ inches (80 cm). Check your door width and adjust as needed

MAKING THE DRAFT STOPPER

Step 1: Measure and cut three pieces of fabric as follows:

Back piece: 39½ x 8 inches (100 x 20 cm)

Front piece: 33½ x 8 inches (85 x 20 cm)

Handle: 4 x 8 inches (10 x 20 cm) (This is to make an optional handle for hanging the stopper when it's not being used.)

DRAFT STOPPER CONTINUED

Step 2: Take the back piece and hem one of the short edges. To do this, fold ⅜ inch (1 cm) of fabric to the wrong side, press, fold another ⅜ inch (1 cm) of fabric to the wrong side, press again, and stitch in place near the first fold. (Fig. 1)

From the hemmed edge, fold the fabric back over onto itself, with right sides together, by 4¾ inches (12 cm). Press the fold but do not sew it yet because it will eventually be the buttonhole flap for the closure.

Step 3: Take the front piece and hem one of the short edges as you did with the back piece in Step 2. (Fig. 2)

Step 4: Fold the handle piece in half lengthwise, right sides together. Pin and sew the long raw edges together, leaving the short ends unstitched. Turn to the right side and press. Place the handle piece on the right side of the back piece, approximately 4 inches (10 cm) from the unhemmed end. Line up the raw fabric edges. (Fig. 3)

Step 5: Pin the back and front pieces together with right sides facing; align the unhemmed ends and leave the short hemmed ends unpinned. (Fig. 4)

Join the front and back pieces by sewing along one long side (starting from the front piece hemmed end), down the short unhemmed end, and along the other long side (stopping at the other side of the front piece hemmed end).

Leave the hemmed ends open for the stopper insert. Turn the whole piece right side out.

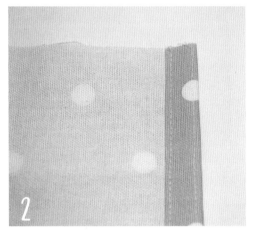

Use a round-ended object to push the corners out neatly.

On the buttonhole flap of the back piece, you'll need to finish the unstitched sides. To do this, fold the fabric to the wrong side, so the folds line up with the seam allowances on the sides, and then topstitch in place approximately ⅕ inch (½ cm) from the fold.

Step 6: Mark two buttonholes on the buttonhole flap, approximately 1¼ inches (3 cm) in from the edges. Once you're happy with the placement, use your sewing machine to make the buttonholes. We recommend making a buttonhole on a spare piece of fabric first to practice the technique and to make sure that your chosen button will fit through the hole.

Step 7: Use a seam ripper to cut your buttonholes open. Start at one end and cut to the middle and then turn and repeat at the other end. This gives a flawless cut to the buttonhole. (Fig. 5)

Step 8: With the cover right side out, fold the flap so it sits over the front piece. Insert a pencil into each buttonhole to mark the position on the front piece. Hand-stitch the buttons in place at the marks. (Fig. 6)

Step 9: To make the stopper insert, use a piece of spare fabric approximately 33 x 13¾ inches (84 x 35 cm). Fold it in half lengthwise, seam the length and one side, turn it right side out, stuff it with polyester fiberfill or old socks, and then stitch the end closed.

Step 10: Place the insert inside the draft stopper to finish.

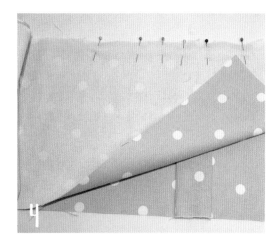

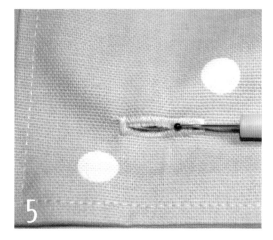

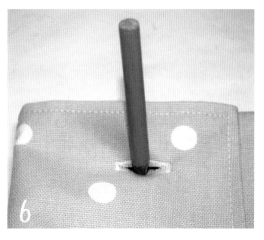

CREATIVE SPACES

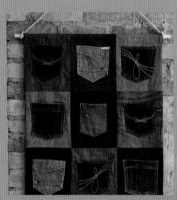

The main living spaces of your house shouldn't be the only ones getting dressed up. Let's organize and freshen up the rest of the house with some fabulous fabrics.

FABRIC COVERS

GIVE YOUR SEWING ROOM A MAKEOVER

Innovative ways to spruce up your
sewing room with beautiful
fabrics and practical ideas.

Designer: Rebecca Reid **Styling:** Louise Day **Photography:** Philip Sowels

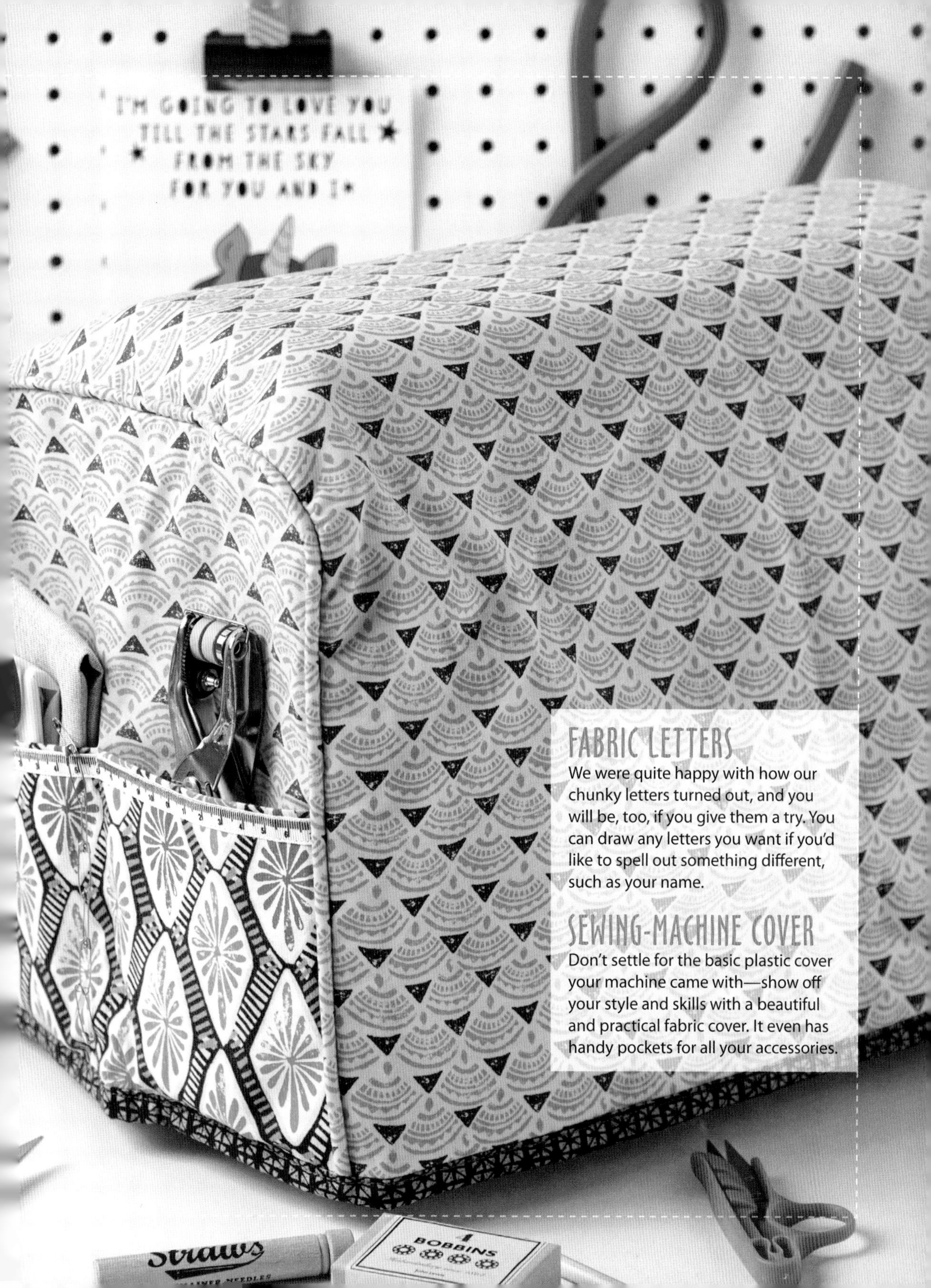

I'M GOING TO LOVE YOU
TILL THE STARS FALL ★
FROM THE SKY
FOR YOU AND I★

FABRIC LETTERS

We were quite happy with how our chunky letters turned out, and you will be, too, if you give them a try. You can draw any letters you want if you'd like to spell out something different, such as your name.

SEWING-MACHINE COVER

Don't settle for the basic plastic cover your machine came with—show off your style and skills with a beautiful and practical fabric cover. It even has handy pockets for all your accessories.

Straws

BOBBINS

SEWING PINAFORE

We like to wear a cover-up when we're sewing (even if it's an old sweatshirt) so tiny fibers and threads don't stick to our clothes. We also have a habit of pinning needles and pins to our clothes and forgetting to take them out before they're washed, so a pinafore really helps.

CORD ORGANIZER

Wrap your trailing sewing machine cords in this neat little organizer and store it in the machine cover's pocket when you're done for the day. It has to be the ultimate in sewing room tidiness!

SEWING-MACHINE COVER

YOU WILL NEED

- Main fabric, see instructions for size
- Pocket fabric, see instructions for size
- Binding fabric, see instructions for size
- Interlining fabric, see instructions for size
- Lining fabric, see instructions for size
- Printed tape or ribbon, see instructions for size
- Piping cord, see instructions for size
- Matching sewing thread

MEASUREMENTS

The finished sewing-machine cover will fit your machine.

NOTE: Use a ⅗-inch (1½-cm) seam allowance, unless otherwise instructed.

MEASURING AND CUTTING

Step 1: To make your cover fit your sewing machine exactly, measure it and make note of the following:

- **Height** (from the base of the machine to the top)
- **Length** (from the open side to the handle side, across the front of the machine)
- **Around your machine** (from the base of the machine at the front, up over the top of the machine, and down to the base of the machine at the back, making sure you include any knobs or wheels that extend out from the main body)

Step 2: Cut the fabric to the following sizes:

- **Main body:** the measurement around your machine plus 1¼ inches (3 cm) by the length plus 2½ inches (6 cm). Cut one piece each from the main fabric, the interlining, and the lining fabric.
- **Sides:** the height of your machine plus 1¾ inches (4½ cm) by the depth plus 2½ inches (6 cm). You can curve the top edges if you like, but you need to make sure that the total measurement of the sides and top edge of this piece match the "around your machine" edge of the main body fabric piece. You may need to slope the sides to make it fit. Cut two pieces each from the main fabric, the interlining, and the lining fabric.
- **Pockets:** the depth measurement by half the height of your side fabric plus ⅗ inch (1½ cm). Cut two pieces each from the pocket fabric and the lining fabric.
- **Piping strip:** to match the total measurement of the sides and top of the side piece by 1½ inches (4 cm) wide. Cut two strips from the main fabric.

- **Piping:** cut two pieces of piping cord to the same length as the piping cord strip.
- **Binding:** 1½ inches (4 cm) wide by twice the depth plus twice the length plus 4 inches (10 cm) for ease and turnings (it needs to be long enough to go all around the bottom edge of your cover). Cut one strip from the binding fabric.

MAKING POCKETS

Step 1: Take the main body piece in the main fabric and place the main body interlining piece on the wrong side. Stitch together around all four sides, ⅜ inch (1 cm) in from the edges. Repeat this process to join interlining to the two side pieces of the main fabric. (Fig. 1)

Step 2: Take one pocket piece and place right sides together with one pocket lining piece. Stitch together along the top edge. Turn right sides out so the wrong sides are together and press. Topstitch the tape or ribbon along the top edge. Repeat with the other pocket and lining pieces. (Flg. 2)

Step 3: Take one pocket and place it on top of one interlined side piece in the main fabric. Line up the lower raw edges and then line up the sides. Stitch in place down one side, across the bottom, and up the other side. If you want, stitch a vertical line down the center to divide the pocket in two. Repeat with the other pocket on the other side piece in the main fabric. (Fig. 3)

ADDING PIPING

Step 1: Fold one of the piping strips around one length of piping cord. Match up the long raw edges and then stitch together ⅜ inch

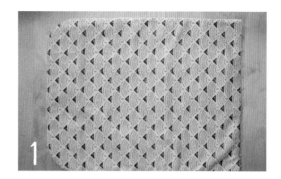

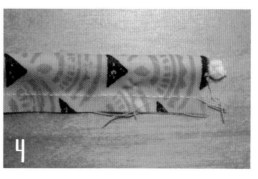

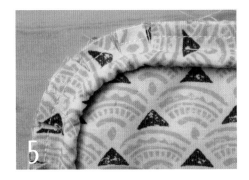

(1 cm) from the edge. Repeat with the other piping strip and length of cord. (Fig. 4)

Step 2: Take one side piece in the main fabric and pin the piping strip around the sides and top edge. Make sure you line up the raw edges and clip the piping strip at the corners so it curves around neatly. Tack the piping strip into place. Repeat with the other side piece and piping strip. (Fig. 5)

Step 3: Place one of these side pieces right sides together with one side of the interlined main body piece. Stitch together, using a zipper foot and stitching as close to the covered piping cord as you can for a neat finish. Repeat with the other side piece on the other side of the main body piece. (Fig. 6)

FINISHING AND BINDING

Step 1: Construct the lining cover in the same way, using the lining pieces. Place the lining cover inside your main cover with wrong sides together. Line up the bottom edges carefully and pin.

Step 2: Take your binding strip and fold over one short end by ⅗ inch (1½ cm) to the wrong side. Press. Starting from this neatened end, pin the strip right sides together with the main cover, pinning through the lining cover, too. Stitch together through all the layers around the bottom edge, using a ⅜-inch (1-cm) seam allowance. When you reach the end, overlap the end by ⅜ inch (1 cm), as shown, trimming off excess fabric if needed. (Fig. 7)

Step 3: Fold the binding strip over to the lining side and then fold the raw long edge by ⅜ inch (1 cm) to the wrong side for a neat edge. Pin in place and then topstitch to finish. (Fig. 8)

FABRIC LETTERS

YOU WILL NEED

- Main fabric, see instructions for size
- Contrast fabric, see instructions
- Soft toy stuffing (such as polyester fiberfill)
- Matching sewing thread

Notes: To create the letter templates, you can either choose a font and print it out or draw letters by hand to the size you want. Try to avoid complicated shapes; rounded edges work well. Cut out the letters from paper to form templates.

Seam allowances are ⅗ inch (1½ cm).

Repeat these steps to make more letters and spell out a special word or even your name.

CUT OUT THE SHAPES

Step 1: Place your paper letter template onto the wrong side of your piece of main fabric (this should be approximately 1½ inches [4 cm] bigger than your letter shape). Trace all the way around the letter shape. Next, flip the letter template over and repeat the process, drawing around it onto the wrong side of another piece of main fabric. (Fig. 1)

Step 2: Cut out your letter shapes, ⅕ inch (½ cm) outside the drawn lines all the way around. You will need this narrow seam allowance so that the gusset will fit more easily around the curves of the letter. (Fig. 2)

ADDING THE GUSSET

Step 1: Cut a gusset strip of contrast fabric to 2 inches (5 cm) wide and long enough to go all the way around your letter, plus 2 inches

(5 cm) for the overlap. Fold one short end to the wrong side by ⅗ inch (1½ cm). Place the gusset strip right sides together with one fabric letter shape and stitch together all the way around. Stitch very slowly and carefully around each of the curves and corners. (Fig. 3)

Step 2: When you get back to where you started, fold the other short end to the wrong side by ⅗ inch (1½ cm) as before, making sure the two ends overlap by ⅘ inch (2 cm)—this is the gap where you will stuff your letter. (Fig. 4)

Step 3: Take the other fabric letter and place it right sides together with the other side of the gusset and stitch it into place. It's important that this letter matches up exactly with the other letter, so pin it in a few places to ensure that your gusset isn't twisted. (Fig. 5)

FINISHING

Step 1: Turn your fabric letter right sides out through the gap in the gusset and press the seams. Stuff your letter by pushing the stuffing through the gusset gap and easing it up into the letter as you go so that it is firmly stuffed. Slip-stitch the gap closed to finish. (Fig. 6)

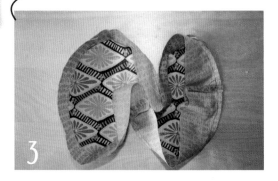

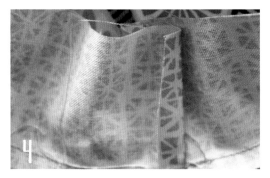

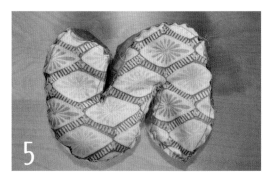

CORD ORGANIZER

Fabric collections with a sewing theme would look great for these sewing-room projects. There are loads to choose from; we particularly like those with retro-style drawings.

YOU WILL NEED

- Main fabric, see instructions for size
- Contrast fabric, see instructions
- Interlining or quilt batting, see instructions for size
- Velcro sew-on hook-and-loop tape, 1½ inches (4 cm) long
- Matching sewing thread

MEASUREMENTS

The finished organizer will be sized to fit your cords and keep them in place.

Note: Seam allowances are ⅗ inch (1½ cm).

MAKING THE CORD ORGANIZER

Step 1: You will use your organizer to hold your sewing-machine cords together so, to measure, loop the cords and tie them together. Measure around the circumference and add 1½ inches (4 cm) for overlapping; this will be the length of your front/back piece. For the width, measure the thickness of the cords so that the cords reach out either side a little bit. Cut two pieces of the main fabric to these measurements. Trim the corners into curves and then cut your interlining to the same size.

Step 2: Place one of your front/back pieces wrong side up, place the interlining on top of that, and then place the other front/back piece of fabric right side up on top of the interlining. Stitch the three layers together around the outside using a machine zigzag stitch. (Fig. 1)

Step 3: For a decorative effect, switch to a straight stitch and work lines of machine quilting though all of the layers. We stitched a diamond pattern by working diagonal lines in one direction and then in the other direction. (Fig. 2)

Step 4: Cut a strip of your contrast fabric to 1½ inches (4 cm) wide and long enough to go all the way around your piece, plus 2 inches (5 cm) for the overlap. This will form your binding. Use the strip to bind the raw edges of your organizer, using the same method as given in the Finishing and Binding section of the sewing-machine cover project. (Fig. 3)

Step 5: To hold the organizer together, stitch the hook half of the Velcro hook-and-loop tape to one end of your organizer and the loop half to the other side of the opposite end of your organizer. You can now wrap it around your cords and fasten it into place. (Fig. 4)

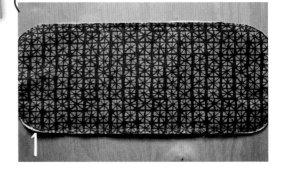

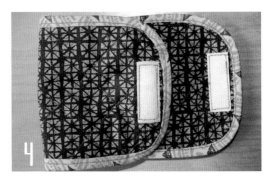

IRONING-BOARD ORGANIZER

YOU WILL NEED

- Main fabric, 28 x 18 inches (71 x 46 cm)
- Contrast fabric, 8 x 21½ inches (20 x 55 cm)
- Bump interlining, 27 x 8 inches (68 x 20 cm)
- Matching sewing thread

MEASUREMENTS

The finished pocket measures 27 x 8 inches (68 x 20 cm).

Note: Use a ⅗-inch (1½-cm) seam allowance throughout.

CUTTING

Step 1: From the main fabric, cut two pieces measuring 28 x 9 inches (71 x 23 cm). From the contrast fabric, cut two pocket pieces measuring 8 x 9 inches (20 x 23 cm), and one handle piece measuring 3½ x 7 inches (9 x 17 cm).

MAKING THE MAIN BODY

Step 1: Take one piece of the main fabric and fold all four edges over by ⅗ inch (1½ cm) to the wrong side. Place the interlining on the wrong side of this piece, underneath the folded edges. (Fig. 1)

Step 2: Take your other piece of main fabric and fold all four edges over by ⅗ inch (1½ cm) to the wrong side, as before. Place this piece right side up on top of the interlining. Line up the edges carefully and pin. Topstitch the layers together around all four edges. (Fig. 2)

Step 3: Sew quilting lines through the layers to help hold them in place and to decorate. To do this, machine-stitch straight lines along the length at regular intervals; we spaced our lines approximately 1¼–1½ inches (3–4 cm) apart. (Fig. 3)

ADDING THE HANDLE AND POCKETS

Step 1: Take the handle piece of fabric and fold in half lengthwise with right sides together. Stitch across one short edge and then down the long raw edge. Turn right sides out. Fold the remaining short raw end inside the fabric tube by ⅗ inch (1½ cm) and topstitch in place. Press. Pin to the center of your quilted organizer, across the width. Sew the ends of the handle into place by stitching a rectangle with a cross in the center at each end of the piece. (Fig. 4)

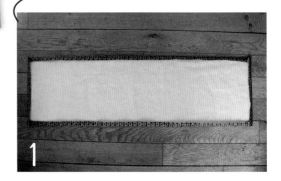

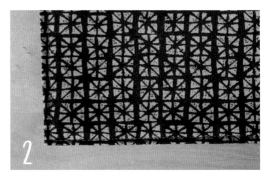

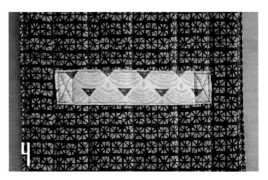

Step 2: Take one pocket piece and fold over one long side by ⅗ inch (1½ cm) to the wrong side, then fold again by ⅘ inch (2 cm). Stitch this hem into place with two rows of topstitching, approximately ⅕ inch (½ cm) apart. Repeat this with the other pocket piece. (Fig. 5)

Step 3: Take one pocket piece and fold over the raw sides and lower edge by ⅗ inch (1½ cm) to the wrong side. Press. Place this pocket over the end of your main organizer piece, lining up the bottom of the pocket with the end of the organizer. Make sure the sides line up as well. Stitch in place down one side, across the bottom, and up the other side. Next, stitch three vertical lines to form the pockets. Repeat with the other pocket piece at the other end of the organizer to finish. (Fig. 6)

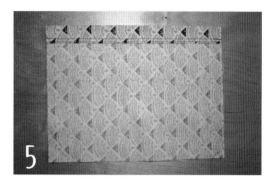

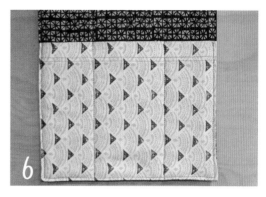

The handle makes the organizer easy to move back and forth from sewing desk to ironing board.

IRONING-BOARD COVER

YOU WILL NEED

- Main fabric, see instructions for size
- Elastic, ⅕-inch (½-cm) wide and long enough to fit around your cover
- Ironing board padding (optional), see instructions for sizing
- Matching sewing thread

MEASUREMENTS

The finished cover will fit over your ironing board.

CUTTING

Step 1: First make a template of your ironing board. You can do this by placing your ironing board upside down over a large sheet of paper (try using a roll of spare wrapping paper, or sheets of paper taped together). Draw around the ironing board and then cut out the shape. This will be your paper template.

Your piece of main fabric needs to be 6 inches (15 cm) larger than your paper template all the way around (this is for the casing, the board lip, and to wrap underneath).

Step 2: Pin your paper template to the wrong side of your piece of main fabric and draw a line roughly 6 inches (15 cm) outside the template all the way around. Measure more closely at the curved end so that your curve is accurate. (Fig. 1)

Step 3: Cut out your fabric along the line you've drawn. (Fig. 2)

Make sure that any wadding you use is heat resistant. You don't want it to melt when you start doing your ironing!

MAKING THE CASING

Step 1: Fold the raw edge of your fabric to the wrong side by ⅗ inch (1½ cm) and then by ⅗ inch (1½ cm) again, all the way around to form a casing for your elastic. At the curved edges, you will need to make small, neat folds to ease the folds into place. Stitch down the casing all the way around, but leave a 1½-inch (4-cm) gap in the center of the straight top edge. (Fig. 3)

Step 2: Attach a safety pin to one end of your elastic. Insert the safety pin into the 1½-inch (4-cm) gap in your elastic and thread all the way around the casing. Tie the two ends of the elastic into a knot to secure. (Fig. 4)

FITTING YOUR COVER

Step 1: If your ironing board isn't already padded, then cut a piece of quilt batting that is 2 inches (5 cm) larger all around than the top of your board. Place the batting on top of your board.

Alternatively, you can just keep your old cover on your ironing board as the padding. If you need new padding or just want some extra thickness beneath your new cover, you can buy specially made ironing-board padding, which you can cut to fit your board, online (try Amazon). Or, if you have an old wool blanket, you can use a couple of layers of it for your padding. (Fig. 5)

Step 2: Place your cover on top of your padded ironing board and pull the elastic tightly so that the cover fits snugly around it. Ease the gathers for an even look and then tie a new knot in the elastic to secure. (Fig. 6)

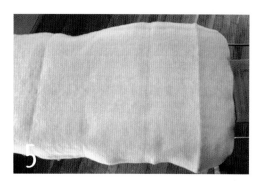

SEWING PINAFORE

YOU WILL NEED

- Main fabric: 35 x 62 inches (90 x 156 cm)
- Contrast fabric: 12½ x 50 inches (32 x 126 cm)
- Matching sewing thread

MEASUREMENTS

The finished pinafore measures 33 x 47 inches
(85 x 120 cm).

Note: Seam allowances are ⅗ inch (1½ cm).

CUTTING

Step 1: From the main fabric, cut one pinafore
piece measuring 35 x 50 inches (90 x 126 cm), plus
two strap pieces measuring 6 x 21 inches (15 x 53 cm)
each. From the contrast fabric, cut one facing piece
measuring 3½ x 50 inches (9 x 126 cm), plus one
pocket piece measuring 10 x 9 inches (26 x 23 cm).

MAKING STRAPS

Step 1: Take one strap piece and fold it in half
lengthwise with right sides together. Stitch down
the long raw edge and then turn right side out and
press. Topstitch down both long sides. Repeat with
the other strap. (Fig. 1)

Step 2: Place the pinafore piece right side up,
with the longer sides running horizontally. Place a
pin at the center point of the top long side.
Measure 3½ inches (9 cm) to the left of the pin and
place one strap here, with the right-hand side of
the strap at the 3½-inch (9-cm) mark. Repeat with
the other strap, 3½ inches (9 cm) to the right of the
pin. Line up the raw edges at the top (Fig. 2)

Step 3: Take the free end of the left strap and place it at the top right corner of the pinafore piece, 1¼ inches (3 cm) in from the right-hand edge, lining up the raw end of the strap with the top edge of the pinafore. Pin in place, being careful not to twist the strap. Repeat with the right strap, pinning it to the top left edge. (Fig. 3)

FACING AND HEMMING

Step 1: Take your facing piece and place it right side down on top of the pinafore piece, lining up the top edges and enclosing the straps. Stitch the two pieces together along the top of the pinafore. (Fig. 4)

Step 2: Fold the facing piece over to the back of the pinafore, then fold over the remaining long raw edge of the facing by ⅗ inch (1½ cm) to the wrong side and press. Stitch in place close to the fold to secure the facing and then topstitch along the top edge of the pinafore to neaten and stabilize the straps. (Fig. 5)

Step 3: Fold over the sides and lower edge of the pinafore by ⅗ inch (1½ cm) to the wrong side, then fold over by ⅗ inch (1½ cm) again. Stitch in place to form a double hem. (Fig. 6)

ADDING A POCKET

Step 1: Take the pocket fabric and fold over the lower edge and sides by ⅗ inch (1½ cm) to the wrong side. Press. Fold over the top edge by ⅗ inch (1½ cm) to the wrong side and then fold over again by 1¼ inches (3 cm). Stitch the top edge down with two lines of topstitching, approximately ⅕ inch (½ cm) apart, to add some extra decoration. (Fig. 7)

Step 2: Put your pinafore on carefully and then pin the pocket where you'd like it to sit when it's finished. Take off the pinafore and topstitch the pocket into place down one side, along the bottom, and then up the other side, to finish. (Fig. 8)

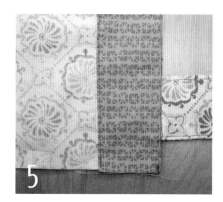

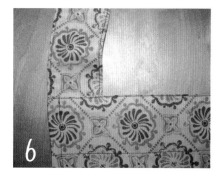

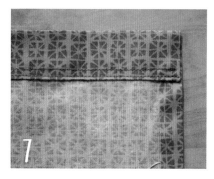

PERFECT POCKETS

UPCYCLE YOUR JEANS

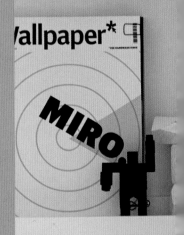

Have a wardrobe clear-out and make Jessica Entwistle's upcycled denim organizer—it'll be great for storing all your sewing odds and ends.

Put your old trousers to good use with this storage idea that's useful and stylish!

WALL ORGANIZER

The great thing about upcycling is that everything you make is unique!

YOU WILL NEED

- Various pairs of old jeans in contrasting blue shades (we used size 12 [UK size 14] and up)
- 1 yard (approximately 1 m) of dark blue cotton fabric (for the backing)
- Matching sewing thread
- Two wooden dowels (ours were 26¾ inches [68 cm] long and ⅝ inch [1½ cm] thick)
- 1¾-yard (1½-m) cord
- Sewing machine fitted with a size 100/16 jeans/denim needle
- Basic sewing kit
- Cutting mat
- Ruler
- Rotary cutter
- Erasable pen

Note: Use a ⅝-inch (1½-cm) seam allowance throughout.

Denim is such a versatile and long-wearing fabric that it almost seems a shame to only wear it! For this project, we've mixed denim shades and jean pockets and used several old pairs of jeans to make a handy hanging wall organizer in a classic nine-patch design. It's great for keeping your sewing kit or accessories neat and tidy.

To make our organizer, we used a jeans/denim sewing-machine needle, which is perfect for stitching on denim because it's stronger than an ordinary needle and also has a very sharp point. You'll find it much easier to sew through all of those pocket layers with one of these needles. Your sewing machine's manual will tell you how to change the needle if you haven't done it before.

Step 1: Our hanging is made from four pairs of old jeans and an old denim shirt, which gave us four pairs of jean pockets and one denim-shirt pocket. (Fig. 1)

First, cut out the pockets from your jeans and then trim close to the edges of the cut pockets but not the pockets themselves. Turn each pocket over and cut away the excess fabric from the back but be sure to leave the edges intact. You want to have just the front decorative part of the pocket left. Hand-sew the buttonhole on the shirt pocket closed and sew a button on top. (Fig. 2)

Step 2: The size of your patches may be dictated by how much fabric you have from your jeans. Our nine-patch design has three central pieces that are 7⅞ x 9¾ inches (20 x 24 cm) each and six pieces for the top and bottom rows that are 7⅞ x 12¼ inches (20 x 31 cm) (these pieces are longer than those in the middle row to take into account the dowel rods' thickness, and they will look the same length when the dowels are in and the wall organizer is hung up).

From the denim fabric from your jeans and shirt, cut six pieces, each measuring 9⅛ x 13⅜ inches (23 x 34 cm), for the top and bottom rows. Cut three pieces, each measuring 9⅛ x 10⅝ inches (23 x 27 cm), for the center row. Number the nine pieces and pockets so you will remember which order to put them in when you start sewing (you can take photos of your preferred pocket placement to remind you, too), (Fig. 3)

Step 3: Place pieces 1 and 2 from the top row right sides together and then stitch down one long edge. (Fig. 4)

Stitch pieces 2 and 3 together in the same way to create the top row. Repeat these steps with the central row (pieces 4, 5, and 6) and bottom row (pieces 7, 8, and 9). These are the three rows of your hanging organizer. (Fig. 5)

Step 4: Turn your rows over and press the seams open. With right sides facing, pin the top strip to the middle strip and sew them together, making sure to match the seams. Next, pin the bottom strip to the middle strip, right sides facing, and stitch together. Turn over your now-sewn nine-patch design and press the seams open. (Fig. 6)

Step 5: Iron your backing fabric and place it flat on the table (or floor). Then, with right sides facing, lay your nine-patch on top. Pin together along the two long edges. (Fig. 7)

Sew along these two outer seams but don't sew the two short seams at this stage. Turn your wall hanging right side out and press flat. (Fig. 8)

Step 6: With the erasable pen, draw a line 9⅞ inches (25 cm) up from the seam where rows 1 and 2 join, and 9⅞ inches (25 cm) down from the seam joining rows 2 and 3. (Fig. 9)

Step 7: Turn the raw top edge of both the joined front and backing fabric over by ⅝ inch (1½ cm). (Fig. 10)

Now turn the top edge over again so it meets the erasable pen line. Check that your dowel fits easily though this fold because it's simple to adjust at this stage to make the turned-over casing wider

or narrower if need be. If you are happy with how it looks, sew along this seam and press. Repeat for the other unsewn edge.

Step 8: Pin your pockets in place—ours are lined up at the pocket tops and centered within the denim squares. They are positioned 2 inches (5 cm) down from the seam above for rows 2 and 3. The top row is 2⅜ inches (6 cm) down from the top to take into account the dowel's thickness. Stitch the pockets in place by sewing about ¼ inch (½ cm) in from the edge of the pocket (between the two rows of topstitching for most of the pockets). Be sure to backstitch at the top corner of each of the pockets a couple of times to give them strength. (Fig. 11)

Step 9: When all pockets are sewn on and pressed, iron your wall hanging and then insert the top and bottom wooden dowels. Tie the cord around both ends of the top dowel and tape the loose ends of the cord to the dowel on both sides so that it sits flat inside the wall hanging. (Fig. 12)

MORE POCKET IDEAS...

1. This design can easily be adapted into a quilt or floor mat for a baby or toddler by removing the pockets—just add batting for warmth and padding if needed, and change the backing to a fleece material.

2. You could change the layout and make a long row of pocket patches to use as a bed organizer or to hang up in a hallway, with each person in the family having his or her own pocket for keys, wallets, and other essentials.

WORK IT!

REVAMP YOUR HOME OFFICE

Stitch coordinated desk
accessories and storage
ideas to create a workspace
that inspires you.

Designer: Rebecca Reid **Styling:** Lisa Jones **Photography:** Jesse Wild

CANVAS BACKPACK

Take your home office out and about with you in this roomy backpack. It has ample space for files, notebooks, and your tech; a zip pocket to stash the essentials; and padded straps for comfort and strength.

DESK ORGANIZER

Our stationery stash is almost as extensive as our fabric hoard, so this organizer is essential for keeping our desks neat. Fill up the sections with clips, pens, washi tape... anything that helps you get creative.

OFFICE ORGANIZER

We love storage that's practical and pleasing to the eye, and this three-pocket organizer, finished with matching fabric trim, meets both of these requirements. We've got no excuse for leaving our paperwork lying around now!

SLOGAN BANNER

We're flying the flag for keeping things neat with this easy-sew slogan banner. Use simple appliqué to stitch a quote that resonates with you and then hang your banner where you can see it to inspire you while you work.

BACKPACK

YOU WILL NEED

- Main fabric: 40 x 58 inches (100 x 147 cm)
- Pocket fabric: 16 x 44 inches (40 x 112 cm)
- Lining fabric: 47 x 44 inches (120 x 112 cm)
- Fusible flexible-foam interfacing: 4¾ x 16½ inches (12 x 42 cm)
- Webbing: taupe, 1½ x 48 inches (30 mm x 120 cm)
- Two sliders (strap adjusters): antique brass, 1½ inches (30 mm)
- Zipper: metal, 22 inches (56 cm)
- Zipper: metal, 12 inches (30 cm)
- Matching sewing thread
- Basic sewing kit

Notes: Use a ⅝-inch (1½-cm) seam allowance.

You will find the printable templates needed to make this project at *www.simplysewingmag.com/101ideas*.

CUTTING

Step 1: Cut the main fabric into the following:

- Zipper pieces: two strips, 3 x 23½ inches (7½ x 60 cm) each.
- Side panel: 5 x 34 inches (13 x 86 cm).
- Straps: two strips, 7⅛ x 17⅜ inches (18 x 44 cm) each.

- Backpack front: 24⅞ x 13¾ inches (63 x 35 cm).
- Backpack back: 18⅞ x 13¾ inches (48 x 35 cm).

  Step 2: Cut the pocket fabric into the following:
- Loop: 3 x 7½ inches (7½ x 19 cm).
- Zipper strips: two strips, 1⅞ x 13½ inches (4½ x 34 cm) each.
- Side panel: 3⅛ x 20⅛ inches (8 x 51 cm).
- Front and back: two pieces, 10¼ x 10¼ inches (26 x 26 cm) each.

  Step 3: Cut the lining fabric into the following:
- Zipper strips: two strips, 3 x 23½ inches (7½ x 60 cm) each.
- Backpack side panel: 5 x 34 inches (13 x 86 cm).
- Backpack front: 24⅞ x 13¾ inches (63 x 35 cm).
- Backpack back: 18⅞ x 13¾ inches (48 x 35 cm).
- Pocket zipper pieces: two strips, 1⅞ x 13½ inches (4½ x 34 cm) each.
- Pocket side panel: 3⅛ x 20⅛ inches (8 x 51 cm).
- Pocket front and back: two pieces, 10¼ x 10¼ inches (26 x 26 cm) each.

MAKING THE PATTERN

Step 1: Trace around the backpack templates on your printed pattern sheet. The templates need to be cut on the fold, so fold the relevant fabric in half wrong sides together and then line up the fold line on the template with the fold of the fabric and pin. Cut around it, leaving the folded edge uncut.

Step 2: Join the lining and outer pieces together for every backpack piece as well as the pocket pieces and side panels (but not the zipper strips or backpack straps). To do this, take an outer piece and its corresponding lining piece, place them wrong sides together, and then machine zigzag-stitch together all the way around the edges to hold

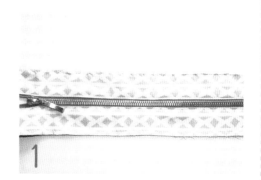

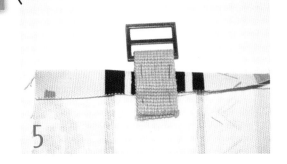

them together and stop them from fraying. Now you can work and stitch with this joined fabric as if it were one piece of fabric.

SEWING THE POCKET ZIPPER AND SIDES

Step 1: Take one main pocket zipper piece and place it right sides together with one lining pocket zipper piece. Sandwich the zipper between them with the long edge of the zipper tape lined up along the top long edges of both pieces. The zipper should be right sides together with the main fabric. Stitch in place using a zipper foot.

Step 2: Turn and press the two fabrics with wrong sides together. Repeat on the other side with the other two main and lining zipper strips and press wrong sides together. Topstitch along both fabric edges on either side of the zipper and then machine-zigzag around the edges to neaten and hold the lining and main fabric together. (Fig. 1)

Step 3: Place one end of the pocket side panel right sides together with the fabric and zipper pieces and stitch together. Repeat at the other end of the side panel and zipper strip to make a loop.

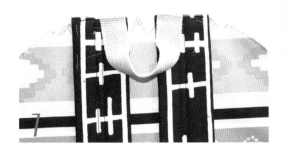

ASSEMBLING THE POCKET

Step 1: Take one lined pocket outer and pin it right sides together with the joined zip and side panel loop, making sure the center of the zip is at the center of the top of the pocket outer. Stitch together all the way around.

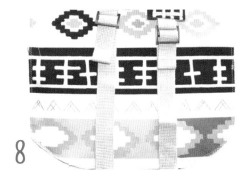

Step 2: Take the other lined pocket outer piece and stitch to the other side of the zipper and side panel. Place the lining side of the pocket side panel together with the outer side of the back panel so you have only lining fabric on the inside of the backpack when it's finished.

ASSEMBLING THE BACKPACK FRONT

Step 1: Take the lined backpack front and sew the two short bottom ends right sides together.

Step 2: Place the pocket inside the inner opening you've created with right sides together. Make sure the center of the zipper lines up with the center of the backpack front and stitch all the way around. (Fig. 3)

Step 3: Join the backpack zipper strips to the longer backpack zipper and then attach the side panel in the same way as for the pocket.

Step 4: Join this zipper and side panel loop to the front backpack piece with right sides together. (Fig. 3)

ATTACHING THE STRAPS

Step 1: Cut the flex foam into two pieces each measuring 2⅜ x 16½ inches (6 x 42 cm).

Step two Take one piece of flexible foam and place it, adhesive side down, centered along the length of the wrong side of one strap fabric piece. Press into place following the package's instructions. Fold one short end over the foam by ¾ inch (2 cm) and pin in place; the other will line up with the top end.

Step 3: Cut a piece of webbing 4 inches (10 cm) long and loop it through the top bar of one slider. Place the two raw ends together

and pin them so they meet up with the raw edges of the turned-under fabric. (Fig. 5)

Step 4: Fold one long strap edge over the top of the foam then fold the other long edge under by ¾ inch (2 cm) and pin in place down the center.

Step 5: Topstitch into place down the center, through all layers of fabric and foam. Topstitch across the short pinned end and then strengthen by stitching a square with diagonal lines running through it. (Fig. 6) Repeat with the other strap.

Step 6: Measure and mark with a pin the midpoint of the top of the backpack back piece. Pin the straps so the inner edge of each is ⅝ inch (1½ cm) away from this center pin and tack.

Step 7: Cut a 7-inch (18-cm) length of webbing for the handle and pin each end on top of the straps, matching raw edges. Tack into place. (Step 7)

Step 8: Cut two 14-inch (35-cm) lengths of webbing. Take one and thread it up through the middle of the two slider bars, over the bottom bar, and then back down. Turn over this short end by ¾ inch (2 cm) and zigzag down to secure. Pin the other end of the webbing to the bottom of the backpack so the strap runs in a straight line down the backpack back. Repeat the process with the other strap. (Fig. 8)

Step 9: Undo the main backpack zipper and then place the backpack back right sides together with the other side of the zipper and side panel and stitch.

Step 10: Turn your backpack right side out through the open zipper to finish.

MAGAZINE FILE

You'll love these fabric files!

YOU WILL NEED

- Main fabric: see instructions for details
- Lining fabric: see instructions for details
- Magazine file
- Metal label holder, gold
- Two paper fasteners, gold
- White glue

CUTTING

Step 1: Start by drawing a template for the outside of your file that you will use to cut out the main fabric. Take a large sheet of paper or newspaper and, starting in the center, trace around the back section of your file and then the sides and front by turning the file over and drawing around it. Draw vertical lines to divide each of the sections.

Step 2: Draw a ¾-inch (2-cm) turning allowance outside this traced line all the way around. Cut your template out along the outer drawn lines but do not cut along the lines dividing the sections.

Step 3: Pin your template onto the wrong side of your main fabric and cut out. Mark the center point of the spine at the top and bottom to help with positioning later. (Fig. 1)

Step 4: Trace over your drawn pattern using the outlines and dividing lines to make separate templates for the lining. From the lining fabric, cut one back, one front, and two sides—you don't need a turning allowance, and make each piece ¼ inch (5 mm) shorter on the top edges.

COVERING THE FILE

Step 1: Mark the center of the back section on the inside of the file. Spread glue onto the back section of the box.

Step 2: Place the back of the file on the center of the wrong side of your fabric, matching center lines, and push firmly into place.

Step 3: Spread glue on the sides and front of the file and then press onto the fabric. When you stick the front into place, fold the short edge under and glue it down. (Fig. 2)

Step 4: Fold the bottom edges under the base of the file and stick down.

Step 5: Make small snips along the curved side edges and then glue them down to the inside of the file. Glue the front and back top edges to the inside at the same time. (Fig. 3)

Step 6: Place the lining pieces inside the file so they meet at the bottom edges but come just below the top edge. Glue in place. (Fig. 4)

FINISHING

Step 1: Attach the metal label holder to the front of your file using paper fasteners through the fabric and magazine file. Punch small holes using sharp scissors.

Step 2: Optional: For a neater finish on the bottom of your file, cut a piece of felt to fit and stick over the fabric edges.

1

2

3

4

BINDER COVER

YOU WILL NEED

- Main fabric: 29 x 45 inches (74 x 115 cm)
- Large pocket fabric: 12 x 21 inches (30 x 52 cm)
- Small pocket fabric: 8 x 21 inches (20 x 52 cm)
- Binding fabric: 7 x 11 inches (18 x 26 cm)
- Magnetic clasp
- Two- or three-ring binder (these measurements are for A4 size)
- Matching sewing thread
- Basic sewing kit

Note: Use a ⅝-inch (1½-cm) seam allowance.

CUTTING

Step 1: Cut the fabric as follows:

- Main fabric: cover outer piece and lining, two pieces 14⅝ x 45 inches (37 x 115 cm) each.
- Large pocket fabric: two pieces 11⅞ x 9⅞ inches (30 x 25 cm) each.
- Small pocket fabric: two pieces 7⅞ x 9⅞ inches (20 x 25 cm) each.
- Binding fabric: pocket binding strips, two strips 1⅝ x 9⅞ inches (4 x 25 cm) each; clasp strip 4 x 4 inches (10 x 10 cm).

MAKING THE POCKETS

Step 1: Place the two pieces of fabric for the large pocket wrong sides together so that the top raw edges are matching.

Step 2: Take one of the binding strips and place it right sides together along the 9⅞-inch (25-cm) edge, matching raw edges. Stitch together all the way along the fabric, using a ⅜-inch (1-cm) seam allowance.

Step 3: Turn the other long edge of the strip under by ⅜ inch (1 cm) and then turn over to the other side of the pocket fabrics and topstitch in place to bind the edge.

Step 4: Repeat this process to make the small pocket. (Fig. 1)

ATTACHING THE POCKETS AND CLASP

Step 1: Fold the clasp strip in half, right sides together, and stitch across the top short end and down the length. Turn right side out and press. Attach the male half of the magnetic clasp to the center of the turned-under short end following the package's instructions.

Step 2: Turn the right-hand side of the large pocket under by ¾ inch (1½ cm) and press.

Step 3: Take the cover outer piece and place it right side up so the longer edges are horizontal. Place the large pocket on the left-hand side so that the raw edges match up on the left side and bottom. Slip the raw short ends of the clasp strip between the right turned-under edge of the pocket and the cover outer piece by ⅝ inch (1½ cm) and centered down the length. Have the clasp side facing up.

Step 4 Topstitch the pocket to the outer only down the turned-under right-hand side, stitching through the clasp strip too to secure. Stitch the bottom and left side down to secure ⅜ inch (1 cm) in from the edge. (Fig. 2)

Step 5: Repeat this with the small pocket but turn under the left-hand side and place it on the opposite side of cover outer, matching up the right-hand sides.

ASSEMBLING THE COVER

Step 1: Place the cover lining and the cover outer piece (with pockets and clasp strip attached) right sides together and stitch all the way around, leaving a turning gap along the center of one long side.

Step 2: Turn right side out through the gap and press the gap's fabric edges under.

Step 3: Place the cover right side down and fold the right-hand edge with the long pocket over to the lining side so that the topstitched right edge of the pocket is on the edge to create a flap. Pin or clip into place.

Step 4: Repeat Step 3 on the left-hand side with the short pocket. (Fig. 3)

Step 5: Topstitch along both long edges to hold the flaps in place and neaten.

Step 6: Put your binder in the flaps and fold the clasp strip over to the front. Mark with a pin where the clasp touches the front cover. Remove the cover and insert the female part of the clasp at the point you marked. (Fig. 4)

Step 7: Slip the ring binder into its new cover. You can slip the back cardboard section of an A4 notepad into the big pocket and keep other sheets of paper in the small pocket.

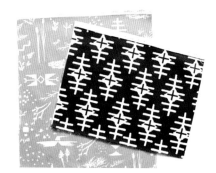

1

2

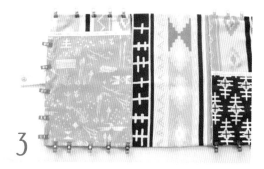

3

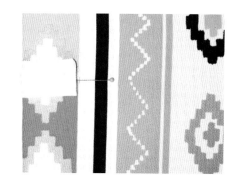

4

DESK ORGANIZER

YOU WILL NEED

- Main fabric: 16 x 18 inches (40 x 45 cm)
- Contrast fabric: 16 x 44 inches (40 x 112 cm)
- Foam-core board: white, 2 sheets, 12 x 16½ inches (30 x 42 cm) each
- Double-sided tape
- Matching sewing thread
- Basic sewing kit

Note: Use a ⅝-inch 1½-cm seam allowance.

CUTTING

Cut the foam-core board as follows:

Tray

Base: 4 x 16½ inches (10 x 42 cm). **Short sides:** two pieces, 4 x 1¼ inches (10 x 3 cm) each. **Long sides:** two pieces, 16½ x 1¼ inches (42 x 3 cm) each. **Long divider (left):** 8¾ x 1¼ inches (22 x 3 cm). **Long divider (right):** 7⅞ x 1¼ inches (20 x 3 cm). **Short dividers:** three pieces, 2 x 1¼ inches (5 x 3 cm) each. **Central divider:** 4 x 1¼ inches (10 x 3 cm).

Cell-phone box

Base: 1⅞ x 3⅜ inches (4½ x 8½ cm). **Short sides:** two pieces, 1⅞ x 2⅜ inches (4½ x 6 cm) each. **Long sides:** two pieces, 3⅜ x 2⅜ inches (8½ x 6 cm) each.

Cut the fabric as follows:

Main fabric—tray

Base: 5¼ x 17¾ inches (13 x 45 cm). **Short sides:** two pieces, 5¼ x 2⅜ inches (13 x 6 cm). **Long sides:** two pieces, 17¾ x 2⅜ in (45 x 6 cm) each.

Contrast fabric—tray

Base: 5¼ x 17¾ inches (13 x 45 cm). **Short sides:** two pieces, 5¼ x 2⅜ inches (13 x 6 cm) each. **Long sides:** two pieces, 17¾ x 2⅜ inches (45 x 6 cm) each. **Long divider (left):** two pieces, 9⅞ x 2⅜ inches)(25 x 6 cm) each. **Long divider (right):** two pieces, 9⅛ x 2⅜ inches (23 x 6 cm) each. **Short dividers:** six pieces, 3⅛ x 2⅜ inches (8 x 6 cm) each. **Central divider:** two pieces, 5½ x 2⅜ inches (13 x 6 cm) each.

Contrast fabric—cell-phone box

Base: two pieces, 3 x 4⅝ inches (7½ x 11½ cm) each. **Short sides:** four pieces, 3 x 3⅝ inches (7½ x 9 cm) each. **Long sides:** four pieces, 4⅝ x 3⅝ inches (11½ x 9 cm) each.

MAKING THE PIECES

Step 1: All of the desk organizer pieces are made in the same way. Starting with the foam-core board piece, main fabric piece, and contrast fabric piece you cut out for the tray base. The main fabric goes on the outside, and the contrast is used to line the inside.

Step 2: Stick double-sided tape around the edge of one side of the foam-core board.

Step 3: Center the foam-core board on top of the wrong side of the main fabric piece with the tape, side up. Remove the strips from the tape and then fold the fabric edges over the board and press down on the tape to hold it in place. (Fig. 1)

Step 4: Place the contrast lining piece right side up on top of the foam-core board you have just folded the fabric over. Turn the edges under so they meet up with the folded-over edges of the outer fabric. Slip-stitch the two fabric edges together all the way around. (Fig. 2)

Step 5: Cover and line each of the foam board pieces in the same way. The outer tray has the main fabric on one side and the contrast fabric as lining. Cover and line the dividers and the cell-phone box with the contrast fabric. (You can use all the same color or a mixture of colors if you prefer.)

JOINING THE PIECES

Step 1: Take a long side piece and a short side piece and place them lining sides together. Work a few small stitches through the outer fabric at one end to anchor your thread and then oversew the two pieces together down the side. You should only stitch through the outer fabric; you'll find it easier if you angle the pieces slightly to keep your stitches barely visible. (Fig. 3)

Step 2: Join the other side pieces together in the same way as in Step 1.

Step 3: Stitch the base to the bottom edges of the four sides to complete your tray.

Step 4: Place the dividers in position inside the tray and slip-stitch them to the tray lining to hold them in place. Refer to the photograph for placement or choose your own arrangement to fit your stationery. (Fig. 4)

Step 5: Make the cell-phone box the same way that you made the tray. You can then put the cell-phone box into the space at the top right of the tray to store your phone while you're working.

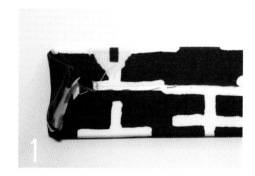

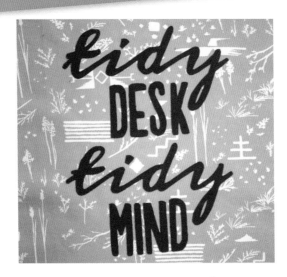

YOU WILL NEED

- Main fabric: 20 x 24 inches (50 x 60 cm)
- Lettering fabric: 11 x 9 inches (28 x 22 cm)
- Paper-backed fusible web (e.g., Wonder-Under, Bondaweb): 11 x 9 inches (28 x 22 cm)
- Heavyweight iron-on interfacing: 20 x 12 inches (50 x 30 cm)
- Wooden dowel: 12 inches (30 cm)
- Cord for hanging
- Matching sewing thread
- Basic sewing kit

Note: You will find the printable template at *www.simplysewingmag.com/101ideas.*

CUTTING OUT THE BANNER

Step 1: Cut your main fabric into two pieces, each measuring 18½ x 12 inches (47 x 30 cm) for the front and back of the banner.

APPLIQUÉING THE LETTERS

Step 1: Trace the banner outline and words from the printed pattern onto tracing paper and then cut around the outline. Place this on the wrong side of your banner front fabric, positioning the bottom of the points ⅝ inch (1½ cm) up from the lower short edge of the fabric and draw around it. Put pins along these drawn lines so you can see the outline from the right side without marking the fabric.

Step 2: Turn your traced pattern over to the wrong side and place your fusible web paper-side up on top of it. Trace over just the letters (not the outline) onto the paper side so you are tracing them in reverse. (Fig. 1)

Step 3: Place your traced fusible web paper-side up onto the wrong side of your lettering fabric and press it gently into place using a dry, medium-temperature iron (don't use steam) until it is firmly stuck.

Step 4: Carefully and accurately cut out all of the letters along your drawn pencil lines and then remove the paper backing from each of them.

Step 5: Place your front banner fabric right sides up and then place the letters on top, referring to the traced template and pinned outline for positioning. Press into place. (Fig. 2)

Step 6: Machine-stitch through the center of each letter to hold them firmly in place and for a decorative effect.

MAKING THE BANNER

Step 1: Remove the pins and then press the interfacing onto the wrong side of the appliquéd fabric; this will give the banner a little more body, which will help it hang better.

Step 2: Place the banner front right sides together with the banner back and then stitch together along all of the drawn lines, leaving a 4-inch (10-cm) gap in the center of the top for turning. Trim ⅜ inch (1 cm) outside the stitching all the way around and clip the points. (Fig. 3)

Step 3: Turn the banner right side out, folding the gap's fabric edges to the inside. Press.

Step 4: Fold the top over by 2 inches (5 cm) to the back and slip-stitch down to make a casing. Be sure to stitch only through the lining so your stitches can't be seen from the front. (Fig. 4)

Step 5: Thread the dowel through then tie cord to each end to hang the banner.

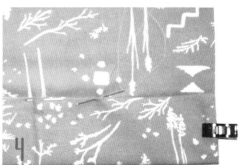

OFFICE ORGANIZER

YOU WILL NEED

- Main fabric: 26 x 22 inches (65 x 54 cm)
- Pocket fabrics: three different fabrics, 7 x 31 inches (17 x 78 cm) each
- Binding fabric: 3 x 36 inches (8 x 90 cm)
- Heavyweight interfacing: 18 x 30 inches (44 x 75 cm)
- 1½-inch (30-mm) webbing, taupe: 48 inches (120 cm)
- Velcro sew-on loop and stick-on hook: 12 inches (30 cm)
- Three metal label holders, gold
- Slx paper fasteners, gold
- Matching sewing thread
- Basic sewing kit

CUTTING

Step 1: Cut the fabric as follows:

Main fabric: organizer front and back, two pieces, 20⅞ x 10⅝ inches (53 x 27 cm) each. **Pocket binding:** three strips, 1⅝ x 10⅝ inches (4 x 39 cm). **Pocket fabric (for each pocket):** two pieces, 6¾ x 15⅜ inches (17 x 39 cm) each. **Binding fabric:** two strips, 1⅝ x 35½ inches (4 x 90 cm) each.

Step 2: From the interfacing, cut the following: **Pockets:** three pieces, 6¾ x 9⅞ inches (17 x 25 cm). **Main body:** 20⅞ x 10⅝ inches (53 x 27 cm).

MAKING THE POCKETS

Step 1: Start by making the top pocket. Place one piece of fabric right side down and then place the interfacing on top so that it is centered across (the fabric will be longer on either side but the same width). Pin the other piece of pocket fabric right side up on top of the interfacing.

Step 2: Bind the top edge of the pocket pieces by placing the binding strip and pocket right sides together. Stitch using a ⅜-inch (1-cm) seam allowance. Topstitch to finish.

Step 3: Stitch webbing across the pocket 1 inch (2½ cm) down from the top. (Fig. 1) Repeat to make the other two pockets.

ATTACHING THE POCKETS

Step 1: Place the organizer front piece right side down, place the interfacing on top, and then place the organizer back piece right side up on top of that. Trim the corners to round them slightly. Stitch together ¼ inch (5 mm) from the edge to hold them securely together.

Step 2: Fold the sides of the bound pockets to give them depth. Mark a line with pins 1⅝ inch (4 cm) from the right short edge all the way down. Mark another line 1¼ inch (3 cm) in from this. Fold the pocket along the first line so that the pocket front is right sides together. Fold the pocket back along the second line to make an accordion (concertina) fold. Press and then tack this fold together along the bottom. Repeat this process on the other side of the pocket. (Fig. 2)

Step 3: Fold the sides of the other two pockets in the same way and tack in place.

Step 4: Lay the interfaced organizer body right side up with the bottom pocket right side down on top so that the bound top points downward and the bottom raw edge is positioned 1⅝ inch (4 cm) up from the lower edge of the organizer body. Stitch the pocket in place all the way along the bottom and through the folds using a ¾-inch (2-cm) seam allowance. (Fig. 3)

Step 5: Fold the pocket upward, press into place, and then tack to the organizer back.

Step 6: Stitch the other two pockets in place in the same way. Place the raw edge of the middle pocket 8¼ inch (21 cm) up from the bottom. Place the raw edge of the top pocket 15 inches (38 cm) from the bottom.

BINDING AND FINISHING

Step 1: Join the two binding strips right sides together along the short ends to make one long strip. Starting at the center of the bottom of the organizer front, bind the edges in the same way as for the top of the pockets, folding and overlapping the short ends and then trimming to fit. Remove all tacking stitches when you're finished. (Fig. 4)

Step 2: Hand-stitch the loop side of the Velcro to the top of the back of the organizer.

Step 3: Place a metal label holder in the center of the tape on each of the pockets by securing with two paper fasteners each. Make your own labels to slide inside the holders.

Step 4: Remove the tape from the back of the Velcro hook and stick it to the edge of your desk or table. You can now hang your organizer by pushing the Velcro together.

LOOK SHARP

A PRETTY PADDED SCISSOR CASE

Keep your sewing scissors
safely tucked away in a
padded floral case by Jennie
Jones. It's a snap to make!

SCISSOR CASE

Keep your scissors handy by storing them safely in this case.

YOU WILL NEED

- 1 fat quarter
- Bias or ribbon: 4¾ inches (12 cm)
- Quilt batting, 2 ounces
- Matching sewing thread
- Basic sewing kit

TEMPLATES

You will find the template needed to make this project on page 189.

Note: Cut out your fabric and stitch using a ⅜-inch (1-cm) seam allowance.

Designer Jennie says, "If, like me, you have your scissors and cutters scattered around the house, this scissor tidy, with three compartments, is just the thing. Keep it next to your sewing machine for easy snipping!"

Step 1: Trace around the template and then use it to cut one piece of batting and two pieces of fabric.

Step 2: Pin the fabric pieces right sides together with the batting underneath. (Fig. 1)

Step 3: Fold the bias or ribbon in half and pin it into place in position on the template.

Step 4: Sew through all layers (and through the ribbon loop) all the way around, leaving a 2-inch (5-cm) turning gap on the longest side.

Step 5: Turn right side out and then fold the edges of the gap to the inside and press. (Fig. 2)

Step 6: Take the longest edge and fold it in so that the top corner meets the edge of the curve and press (this is the first fold). (Fig. 3)

Step 7: Taking the other side, fold it over the first fold and press (the second fold).

Step eight Fold the remaining part back over the first fold so it meets with the second fold and pin into place. (Fig. 4)

Step 9: Topstitch along all of the outside edges to hold the folds in place. Slip your scissors in the pockets to complete.

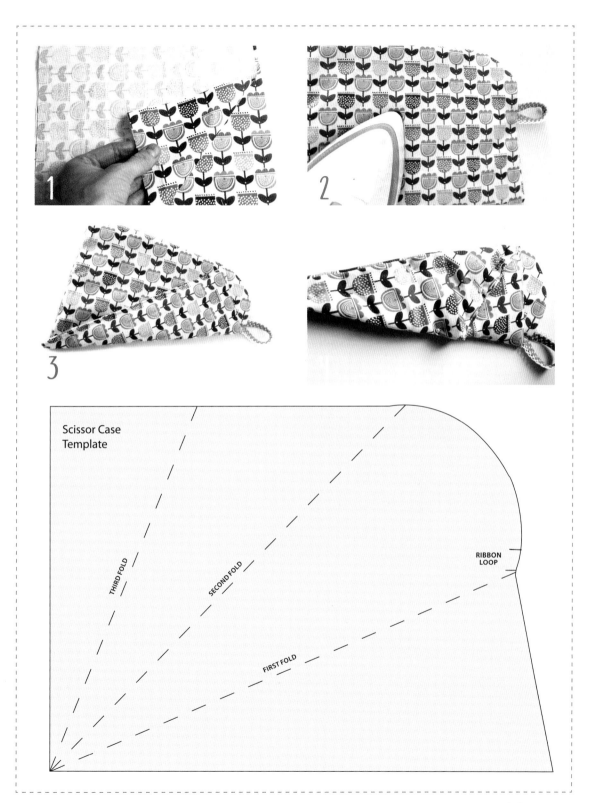

Scissor Case
Template

THIRD FOLD

SECOND FOLD

FIRST FOLD

RIBBON
LOOP

GREAT OUTDOORS

A SET OF AL FRESCO ACCESSORIES

In the garden or on the beach,
deck-chair stripes are the
way to go for your outdoor
accessories!

Designer: Rebecca Reid **Styling:** Louise Day **Photography:** Philip Sowels

DUFFEL BAG

Gather up everything you need for a day outdoors in this jaunty duffel bag. If the sun doesn't shine, the bag will brighten up the day instead! To line the bag, we used the same waterproof fabric as for the picnic-blanket backing.

DECK-CHAIR SLING AND HEADREST

Make over a tired deck chair and give it an extra-comfy head cushion—perfect for lounging with a book and a cold drink. This project is so simple, you'll wonder why you've never sewn your own before.

DECK-CHAIR STRIPES

WINDBREAK WITH A POCKET

Windbreaks are a must for a breezy summer, so make yours stand out by choosing bold stripes. And to make it doubly useful, sew in a pocket to keep handy items like sunblock or a good book close by.

PICNIC BLANKET

Backed with waterproof fabric—a breathable polyurethane in dark navy—this throw is very practical as well as stylish. The contrasting striped edging is in the same fabric as the deck chair to make it feel like part of a set.

GARDEN CUSHION

Try some quilting on this comfy cushion that you can take anywhere!

YOU WILL NEED

- Main fabric: 31 x 42 inches (79 x 106 cm)
- Polyester fiberfill: 2¼–4²/₅ pounds (1–2 kg)
- Matching sewing thread
- Strong cotton/upholstery thread

MEASUREMENTS

The finished cushion measures 20 x 20 x 4 inches (50 x 50 x 10 cm)

Note: Use a ³/₅-inch (1½-cm) seam allowance throughout and press all seams open as you go.

MAKING THE CUSHION

Step 1: Cut out the following pieces:

- Two back/front pieces, 21 x 21 inches (53 x 53 cm) each
- Four side gussets strips, 5¹/₁₀ x 21 inches (13 x 53 cm) each

Step 2: Take two of the side strips and place them right sides together. Stitch along the short edges, starting and finishing ³/₅ inch (1½ cm) from each end; this will make joining them to the top and bottom neater. Repeat this with the other two side strips and then join the two long strips to form a continuous loop. (Fig. 1)

Step 3: Place the cushion front right sides together with one long edge of the side strip, lining up the side seams with the corners. Pin into place. Starting ⅗ inch (1½ cm) in from the corner, stitch together, stopping ⅗ inch (1½ cm) from the other corner but leaving the machine needle inserted into the fabric layers. Raise your machine foot and pivot the fabrics so you can continue stitching down the next side. Continue joining the side strips to the front all the way around, always starting and finishing ⅗ inch (1½ cm) from each end. (Fig. 2)

Step 4: Stitch the cushion back to the other long edge of the side strip, with right sides together, in the same way but this time leave a 6-inch (15-cm) turning gap in the center of one side. (Fig. 3)

Step 5: Turn your cushion cover right side out. Stuff quite firmly, pushing the stuffing into the corners. Slip-stitch the gap closed. (Fig. 4)

Step 6: Mark the points on the front of the cushion for the quilting indent stitches. There are nine of them in a three-by-three grid, and you should space them evenly across the cushion front, 5 inches (12½ cm) apart. Push pins through the cushion front at these points. Repeat on the cushion back to mark the same points.

Step 7: Thread your needle with a strong cotton or upholstery thread. Push the needle through the cushion front about 2 inches (5 cm) from the center pin and then pull it up again at the pin, leaving a short end of thread still coming out of the fabric. Work a couple of small stitches in the fabric here to secure it and

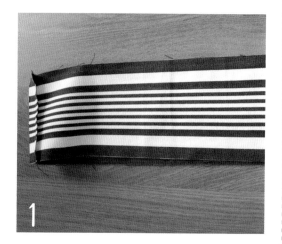

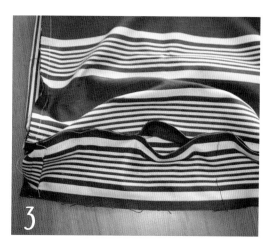

then snip off the tail end flush with the fabric. Push the needle down through the cushion and out at the center pin on the back, pulling the thread all the way through. Work another few stitches through this center point to pull the cushion together and form an indent. Work a few small stitches to secure the thread and then snip it off. Repeat this process with the remaining eight points. (Fig. 5)

Step 8: You can now quilt the edges of the cushion, again using strong cotton thread. Anchor your thread at one corner, ⁴⁄₅ inch (2 cm) down from the top, in the same way as before. Push the needle diagonally up to the cushion front, ⁴⁄₅ inch (2 cm) from the corner. Work a ¼ inch (½ cm) stitch, then push the needle diagonally back through to come out at the cushion side, ⁴⁄₅ inch (2 cm) across and down from the cushion top. Work another ¼ inch (½ cm) stitch, then bring the needle out again at the cushion front, ⁴⁄₅ inch (2 cm) up and across from the side. You may find it helps to measure a whole side and mark these stitch positions with pins before you stitch it.

Step 9: Repeat this process along all four sides of the cushion front, pulling the stitches reasonably tight to make the cushion look quilted. Repeat the whole process with the cushion back and the other side edge. (Fig. 6)

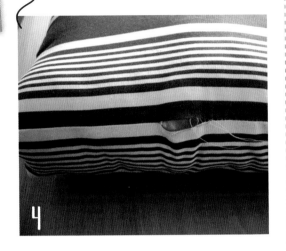

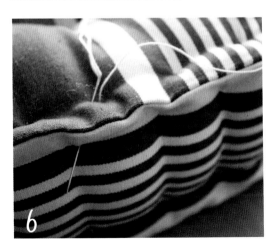

WINDBREAK

YOU WILL NEED

- Main fabric: 59 x 118 inches
  (150 cm x 300 cm)
- Pocket fabric: 13 x 17 inches (33 x 43 cm)
- Four wooden poles
- Matching sewing thread

MEASUREMENTS

The finished windbreak measures 55 x 102
inches (140 cm x 260 cm).

Notes: Use a ⅗-inch (1½-cm) seam allowance
throughout and press all seams open as you go.

You can use poles from a windbreak you
already have or, if you're making a new one, try
using approximimately 71-inch (180-cm)-long
broom handles, which are available from
hardware or home-supply stores. Make sure
the poles or broom handles are longer than
the windbreak's side so there is enough length
to hammer into the sand or grass. You can
sand the ends of each pole into a point so they
are easier to drive into the ground.

MAKING THE MAIN BODY

Step 1: Fold the top long edge of your fabric to the wrong side by ⅘ inch (2 cm) and then 1¼ inches (3 cm) and press. Stitch this hem down and then repeat with the bottom long edge. (Fig. 1)

Step 2: The poles need to slide into casings at the sides of the windbreak and two casings evenly spaced across it. To make one end casing, fold the short end of the fabric to the wrong side by ⅘ inch (2 cm) and then 2½ inches (6 cm) and pin. Check that your pole will fit into the casing and make it smaller or larger if you need to. Stitch the casing in place and then repeat this at the other short end of your fabric. (Fig. 2)

Step 3: Measure 37½ inches (95 cm) from the hemmed side along the top of your fabric and mark with a pin. Place a pin at the bottom edge in the same position. Fold your fabric from one pin to the other pin, with wrong sides together, and press. Next, measure 2¼ inches (5½ cm) from the folded edge and stick a line of masking tape along this point. You will use this to sew against because it's a very easy way to make sure you sew in a straight line. Place pins on either side of the tape to make sure that the stripes of the two layers line up. Stitch just next to the masking tape (not through it) all the way down the folded fabric, through both layers, to form a pole casing. Remove the tape. (Fig. 3)

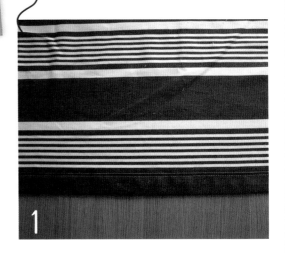

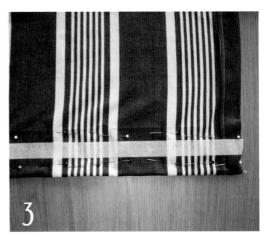

Step 4: Measure 37½ inches (95 cm) from the other hemmed side of the fabric and make another pole casing in the same way.

ADDING A POCKET

Step 1: To make a pocket for your windbreak to hold things while you're on the beach, take your pocket fabric and fold the short sides and long lower edge to the wrong side by ⅘ inch (2 cm). Press. Fold the top long edge to the wrong side by ⅘ inch (2 cm) and then 1¼ inches (3 cm) and stitch down to hem. (Fig. 4)

Step 2: Pin the pocket to the center section of the windbreak, positioning it about 8 inches (20 cm) up from the lower edge and centered between the casings. Stitch into place down one side, along the bottom, and up the other side. If you want to divide the pocket into two sections, stitch a line down the center of the pocket. (Fig. 5)

FINISHING

Step 1: To finish your windbreak, simply slide the poles into the casings. Now you can roll it up to carry it. (Fig. 6)

THE STRIPES COMPANY

Our thanks to The Stripes Company for supplying all of the fabrics for these projects. They sell deck-chair canvas, interior fabrics, oilcloth, and water-repellent fabrics, all by the meter. They also stock a wide range of coordinating trimmings and many ready-made items using their fabrics. Visit *www.thestripescompany.us* to see their whole range.

PICNIC BLANKET

YOU WILL NEED

- Cotton curtain-weight fabric, blue: 57 x 57 inches (145 x 145 cm)
- Binding fabric: 31 x 59 inches (80 x 150 cm)
- Waterproof backing fabric: 57 x 57 inches (145 x 145 cm)
- Matching sewing thread

MEASUREMENTS

The finished picnic blanket measures 57 x 57 inches (145 x 145 cm).

Note: Use a ⅗-inch (1½-cm) seam allowance, unless otherwise stated, and press all seams open as you go.

MAKING THE PICNIC BLANKET

Step 1: Place the waterproof fabric right side down and then place the blue cotton fabric right side up on top. Stitch the two fabrics together around all four sides, using a ⅜-inch (1-cm) seam allowance. This holds the fabrics together and makes binding them much easier. (Fig. 1)

Step 2: Cut the binding fabric into four strips, each measuring 8 x 59 inches (20 x 150 cm). Take one strip and fold it in half along the length, with wrong sides together. Press well and repeat with the other three binding strips. (Fig. 2)

Step 3: Unfold one binding strip and place it right side down. Fold the two long edges over to the wrong side by ⅝ inch (2 cm) and

WATERPROOF FABRIC

It's a good idea to back your picnic blanket with waterproof fabric to keep it dry on top. We've used a breathable polyester fabric coated with PU (polyurethane). It's ideal for clothing and ground cloths, and we've also used it to line the duffel bag to keep the contents dry.

press. Fold the strip in half again along the central crease to enclose the raw edges and press. Repeat with the other three binding strips. (Fig. 3)

Step 4: Take one folded strip and use it to enclose one edge of your joined blue fabric and waterproof fabric. Make sure that the edge of the blanket fabric is inserted right up into the fold in the strip. Pin in place. Feel with your fingers to make sure that the strip's top folded edge and the bottom folded edge are exactly in line and adjust if necessary. Topstitch into place along the edge of the binding strip. Trim the binding strip at both ends so it matches up exactly with the edge of the blanket. Repeat with another binding strip along the opposite side of the throw. (Fig. 4)

Step 5: Take another binding strip and place it over one of the remaining raw edges in the same way as before. This time, fold the short ends to the wrong side by ⅝ inch (2 cm) and trim off any excess binding fabric so the ends are exactly in line with the bound side. Pin in place and then stitch along the length. Repeat with the final binding strip on the opposite side of the blanket. (Fig. 5)

Step 6: Stitch together the side edges of the last two binding strips by hand, using a small slip stitch and thread that matches your binding. (Fig. 6)

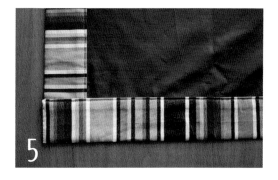

DUFFEL BAG

YOU WILL NEED

- Blue cotton curtain weight fabric: 14 x 57 inches (35 x 145 cm)
- Striped fabric: 17 x 43 inches (50 x 110 cm)
- Waterproof lining fabric: 26 x 57 inches (65 x 145 cm)
- Eight eyelets: silver, ²/₅-inch (11-mm) diameter
- Cotton cord: 98 inches (250 cm)
- Matching sewing thread

MEASUREMENTS

The finished duffel bag measures 24 inches (60 cm) high and 12 inches (30 cm) in diameter

Note: Use a ³/₅-inch (1½-cm) seam allowance throughout and press all seams open as you go.

CUTTING

Step 1: Cut out a 13-inch (33-cm)-diameter circle from paper to make a template for your bag base.

Step 2: From the plain blue fabric, cut the following:

Bag sides: two strips measuring 5 x 43¼ inches (13 x 110 cm)

Base outer: one circle from the template

Step 3: From the striped fabric, cut the following:

Bag outer: 17 x 43¼ inches (43 x 110 cm)

Strap loop: 3½ x 3½ inches (9 x 9 cm)

Step 4: From waterproof fabric, cut the following:

Bag lining: 25 x 43¼ (63 x 110 cm)

Base lining: one circle from the template

MAKING THE BAG

Step 1: Place the long edge of one blue bag side piece right sides together along the long edge of the striped bag outer piece. Stitch together. Repeat with the other blue strip on the opposite side of the striped fabric. Press the seams open. (Fig. 1)

Step 2: Fold this piece in half, right sides together, so the striped fabric meets. Align the raw edges and pin. Take the blue base circle and pin it right sides together with one of the blue ends (this will become the bottom of the outer bag). Pin this in place before you stitch the bag's side seam because you may need to adjust it to fit your circle. Remove a few pins and stitch down the side seam. Keep the pins holding the base in place. (Fig. 2)

Step 3: Make the loop that the cord will go through later. Fold the striped strap loop piece in half with right sides together and stitch down the length. Turn right sides out,

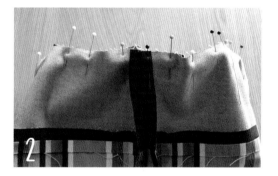

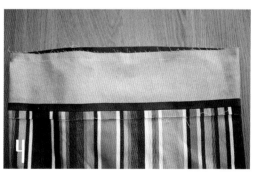

press, and fold in half widthwise, matching up the raw edges. Pin this loop between the bag outer and the bag base, at the side seam, matching up the raw edges. (Fig. 3)

Step 4: Repin the base into place all the way around and then stitch the bag outer and base together, enclosing the loop.

Step 5: Repeat the process in Step 4 to attach the bag lining piece to the base lining piece, but this time leave a 4-inch (10-cm) gap in the center of the lining side seam for turning later.

Step 6: Make sure the bag outer is wrong sides out and the bag lining is right sides out. Place the bag lining inside the bag outer so the right sides are together and match up the side seams. Stitch together all the way around the top edge. Turn the bag right side out through the gap in the lining and then slip-stitch the gap closed. (Fig. 4)

Step 7: Push the lining inside the bag and topstitch around the top edge.

ADDING EYELETS AND CORD

Step 1: Add the eight eyelets around the top. You will insert them into the center of the top blue strip, so measure carefully and insert pins at the positions where you want them, making sure to space them evenly and that the bag's side seams are centered between two eyelets. Follow the instructions on your package of eyelets to cut the fabric and hammer them into place. (Fig. 5)

Step 2: Thread the length of cord in and out of the eyelets, starting and finishing on either side of one of the side seams. Then take one end down through the loop at the base of the bag and knot the two cord ends together to create your strap and drawstring closure. (Fig. 6)

DECK-CHAIR SLING

YOU WILL NEED

- Deck-chair canvas: 18 x 60 inches (45 x 150 cm)
- Striped cushion fabric: 13 x 34 inches (33 x 86 cm)
- Zipper, matching color: 2 inches (⅘ cm)
- Cushion pad, 12 x 16 inches (30 x 40 cm)
- Twill tape: 59 inches (150 cm) (cut into four pieces)
- Matching sewing thread

MEASUREMENTS

The finished deck-chair sling will fit your chair; the finished cushion headrest measures 12 x 16 inches (30 x 40 cm).

Note: Use a ⅗-inch (1½-cm) seam allowance throughout and press all seams open as you go.

MAKING A DECKCHAIR SLING

If you have the old sling for your deck chair, just copy it to make a new one to fit. Some slings have a casing stitched in the top, into which a pole is threaded, while others are stapled on. These instructions are for a pole-threaded sling. For a stapled sling, just remove the staples, cut and hem your canvas to the same size, and then staple the new sling into the same position.

Step 1: Measure the width of your old sling and then fold the long edges of your canvas fabric to the wrong side so it measures the same width. Press and stitch into place. (Fig. 1)

Step 2: Measure the length of your old sling, add 6¼ inches (16 cm) and then cut your canvas to this length. Fold one short end to the wrong side by ⅘ inch (2 cm) and then again by 2½ inches (6 cm) and press. Stitch in place close to the edge to form the casing and then stitch along one short end of the casing. At the other short end, stitch down just ⅘ inch (2 cm) so you have a gap for your pole. Repeat Step 2 at the other end of your canvas. (Fig. 2)

Step 3: Push one casing end through the top of your deck chair and insert the pole. Slip-stitch the ⅘-inch (2-cm) gap closed to hold the pole in place. Repeat this at the bottom of your deck chair with the other end of the sling. (Fig. 3)

MAKING A CUSHION HEADREST

Step 1: Cut your cushion fabric into two pieces, each measuring 13 x 17 inches (33 x 43 cm), and place them right sides together with one short side at the top. Stitch together from the left-hand side for 1½ inches

(4 cm) only, and then stitch together from the right-hand side for 1½ inches (4 cm) only. The gap is where you'll insert the zip next; for now, work long tacking stitches in the gap. (Fig. 4)

Step 2: Open out the joined fabric pieces and place right side down. Press the stitched and tacked seam open. Place your zipper right side down over the tacked gap between the seams and pin into place. Using a zipper foot, stitch the zipper into place close to the teeth. (Fig. 5)

Step 3: Remove the tacking stitches and place right side up. Place two pieces of twill tape on top of each other at the edge with the zipper, ⅕ inch (½ cm) from the seam. Tack into place. Place the other two tape pieces on top of each other at the short end, ⅘ inch (2 cm) in from the raw edge. (Fig. 6)

Step 4: Fold your cushion in half at the zipper, right sides together. Open the zipper halfway. Stitch the fabrics together around the three open sides, enclosing the tape ties as you go. (Fig. 7)

Step 5: Trim the corners of the seam allowance and turn right sides out. Remove the tacking stitches on the ties. Insert the cushion pad and close the zipper. Knot the ties together at the top of your deck chair, around the top of the frame. (Fig. 8)

ESSENTIAL KNOW-HOW

THE GUIDE: STITCHES, TIPS, TECHNIQUES, AND TEMPLATES

Let us walk you through your sewing-kit essentials and explain some terms and techniques.

ROTARY CUTTER

If you want to get into patchwork or dressmaking, a rotary cutter makes short work of cutting out a lot of fabric and pattern pieces. Always cut away from yourself because the cutter is very sharp. You'll need a cutting mat and special ruler to use a rotary cutter.

SCISSORS

Get a large pair of scissors just for cutting fabric. Some are angled so that the bottom blade sits flat to a surface, which is useful for cutting large pieces of fabric. Also buy a small pair of scissors for detail work.

SEAM RIPPER

You'll find this odd-looking tool invaluable for cutting through seams and removing stitches. The hook slips under the stitches while the sharp blade at the back cuts the thread. Replace it when it gets blunt—seam rippers don't cost much.

THREAD

You can hand-stitch with almost any thread, but when using a sewing machine, your thread must be strong enough not to break. All-purpose thread is 100 percent polyester and a good place to start.

TAPE MEASURE

Spend a little extra and get a plastic-coated tape measure that won't stretch to keep your measuring accurate. A tape measure with a metal end is useful for dressmaking, and you can get an extra long one for patchwork.

MARKING TOOLS

Tailor's chalk, water- or air-erasable pens, and pencils make pinning and tacking much easier because you can see where you're supposed to be sewing. They come in different colors to contrast with your fabric.

PINS AND NEEDLES

Indispensable stainless-steel pins have sharp points. Invest in glass-headed pins, too, if you do a lot of sewing. Needles come in many forms; different types are suitable for hand-sewing and machine-sewing.

HOW TO BUY FABRIC

The measurements by which fabric is sold can seem confusing when you first hit the store. If you're buying fabric from a roll (or "bolt"), you'll usually buy it by the yard (36 inches [91 cm]) or meter (39 inches [100 cm]). This is only the length of the fabric you're buying; the width depends on the width of the roll, which can be a yard (91 cm) wide but is also often 44 inches (112½ cm) wide or even sometimes a little wider. Check the information on the end of the cardboard tube inside the fabric or ask someone at the store to measure it for you so you can be sure how much you're buying. You can also buy precut pieces, such as fat quarters, charm packs/squares, and jelly rolls, which save time in measuring and cutting regular shapes and sizes.

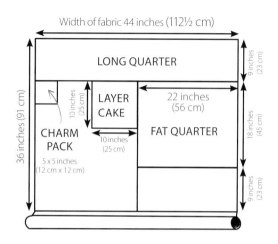

RIGHT AND WRONG SIDES

Sewing is all about knowing which is the right side and which is the wrong side of your fabric. The right side of a piece of fabric is the side you want to be on display when your project is finished. The wrong side is the side that you don't want to see. Following a pattern? It should tell you how you need to place the fabric.

SEAM ALLOWANCES

Most patterns tell you what allowances to use. To sew two fabrics together, you layer them with right sides together and then sew along one side. When you open them up, they will be neatly joined down one side. The excess fabric on the wrong side is called the seam allowance, the width of which depends on where you place your stitch line—the closer to the raw edge you stitch, the narrower the seam allowance.

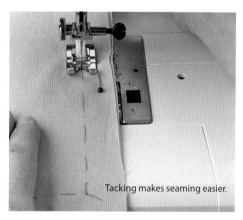

Tacking makes seaming easier.

MACHINE NEEDLE SIZES

Choosing the right needle to suit your fabric.

SIZE	WHAT'S IT USED FOR?
70/10	Delicate fabrics, such as silk and chiffon
80/12	Cotton, linen, wool, polyester
90/14	Cotton, linen, wool, polyester
100/16	Sturdy fabrics, such as canvas, twills, heavyweight wool, heavy linen, and denim
110/18	Sturdy fabrics, such as canvas, twills, heavyweight wool, heavy linen, and denim
Ballpoint or jersey	For jersey and other knitted fabrics; tends to have a blunt tip so it doesn't catch the fine threads
Leather	Has a built-in knife to cut through leather (you will also need a walking foot to slide over the leather or a special presser foot with a Teflon sole)
Industrial	Has a rounded shank at the top (domestic machine needles are flat on one side)

FABRIC TERMINOLOGY

Helping you understand sewing fabric jargon.

	UK, AUS, NZ	US
Calico	Equal weft and warp plain-weave fabric, usually unbleached cotton in different weights; often used for toiles	Cotton fabric with a small floral print
Muslin	Very fine, light, plain-weave cotton fabric	Equal weft and warp plain-weave fabric, usually unbleached cotton in different weights; often used for toiles (or as UK usage)
Muslin gauze	See muslin	Very light, open-weave muslin
Gauze	Extremely soft, fine cotton fabric with a very open plain weave	Any very light fabric, usually plain weave
Cheesecloth	See gauze	Extremely soft, fine cotton fabric with a very open plain weave

CUSHION PAD VARIETIES

Buying the right filling for your cushion can make a big difference to its finished look and feel. Cushion pads are widely available in various shapes, but one of the most popular is the standard square. Cushion pads are filled with either a synthetic or feather filling. Synthetic pads tend to remain plump and spring back into shape, and they are better for those with allergies, while feather-filled pads have a more luxurious, squishier feel. Make note of these standard cushion-pad sizes for future projects.

STANDARD CUSHION PAD SIZES

12 x 12 inches (30 x 30 cm), **14 x 14 inches** (35 x 35 cm), **16 x 16 inches** (40 x 40 cm), **18 x 18 inches** (45 x 45 cm), **20 x 20 inches** (50 x 50 cm), **22 x 22 inches** (55 x 55 cm), **24 x 24 inches** (60 x 60 cm)

AT-A-GLANCE GUIDE TO COMMON FABRIC TYPES

Useful information on fabrics you'll use when sewing homewares and clothes

FIBER NAME	FABRIC TYPES	PROS	CONS	CARE INFORMATION
NATURAL FIBERS				
Cotton	Batiste, broadcloth, calico, corduroy, denim, flannel, seersucker, terry, cotton velvet	Absorbent, cool, strong	Shrinks unless pretreated, some wrinkle badly	Machine wash, tumble dry, can be bleached, use steam iron or iron while damp
Linen	Damask, handkerchief, lawn	Absorbent, cool, strong, very durable	Can shrink, wrinkles	Dry clean to retain crispness or wash to soften
Silk	Chiffon, crepe-de-chine, organza, raw silk, satin, velvet; often found in combination with other fabrics, such as cotton and wool	Absorbent, adapts to body temperature, drapes well	Prone to moth damage, wears along seams, weakened by sunlight and perspiration	Dry clean, although some can be hand-washed; iron on the wrong side at a low temperature
Wool	Crepe, flannel, gabardine, jersey, tweed	Absorbent; warm; flame-, water-, and wrinkle-resistant, provides good insulation	Can shrink, prone to moth damage, knits stretch during wear	Dry clean. although some can be machine-washed; press with a steam iron and a cloth

Useful information on fabrics you'll use when sewing homewares and clothes

FIBER NAME	FABRIC TYPES	PROS	CONS	CARE INFORMATION
SYNTHETIC AND SEMI-SYNTHETIC FIBERS				
Acetate	Satin, silk-like fabrics, taffeta, twill	Silk-like luster, drapes well, dries quickly, low cost	Fades, relatively weak, exhibits static cling, wrinkles	Dry clean or gently machine wash, tumble dry (low), iron low temperature
Acrylic	Double knits, fleece, pile fabrics, wool-like fabrics	Warm, resists wrinkles, mildew, moths, and oily stains	Sensitive to heat, static cling	Machine wash, tumble dry, doesn't need ironing
Nylon	Net, tricot, two-way stretch knits, swimwear	Strong, warm, light weight, resists moths, wrinkles, and mildew	Static cling, holds body heat	Hand or machine wash, tumble dry, iron at a low temperature
Polyester	Cotton, silk- and wool-like fabrics, crepe, double and single knits, fleece, georgette, jersey, velvet, satin taffeta	Strong, warm, very wrinkle-resistant, holds shape and a pressed crease	Static cling, holds body heat	Machine wash, tumble dry, doesn't need ironing
Rayon/ Viscose	Challis, crepe, cotton- and linen-like fabrics, jersey, velvet	Absorbent	Relatively fragile, holds body heat, wrinkles, shrinks	Dry clean or gently machine wash, iron at a moderate temperature, can be bleached
Spandex	Stretch wovens, two-way stretch knits, Lycra (swimwear and activewear fabrics)	Excellent stretch properties, good durability, no static cling	White fabrics might become yellow from prolonged exposure to air	Wash or dry clean

ONE OF A KIND

A quilt is the ultimate handmade home furnishing, and author Kirsty Hartley used photos, drawings, and favorite fabrics to make a unique keepsake for her daughter.

For the ultimate stash-busting project, nothing beats a quilt. But for a truly unique way to use up your treasured scraps, look no further than the beautiful photo quilt that Kirsty Hartley made for her daughter Lila. We're sure you'll be inspired to try something similar once you've read how Kirsty completed this bright and beautiful project.

"I love working with color and with photographic images, and this memory quilt combines the two perfectly. It is particularly special to me, as I made it as a gift for my youngest daughter, Lila, for her fourth birthday.

"I worked on it with her sister and brother, who chose all the photographs and fabrics and helped me to lay it all out and arrange it. We decided to use vibrant, sunny bubblegum shades to match her character.

"It is a rare occasion for me to make something outside of my children's clothing brand, Wild Things, and when I do, it really is a labor of love. Lila carries the quilt everywhere; it has been used to wrap dolls, make [forts], and snuggle on the sofa. I used favorite scraps, Kona solids, and a lovely bamboo-mix batting for softness.

I printed the photographs by making them black and white first (you could also print them in grayscale) and printing them onto washable photo fabric, each piece measuring the width of the paper. I've also added some quotes and little drawings in there.

"A [crib]-sized version of this quilt would make a perfect baby gift. Lila's is quite washed out now, but I hope she will keep it forever."

Kirsty Hartley is the author of *Wild Things: Funky Little Clothes to Sew* and *Wild Things to Make: More Heirloom Clothes and Accessories to Sew for Your Children*. You can see more of Kirsty's work at *www.wildthingsdresses.com*.

TEMPLATES

TEA COZY
Page 106
copy at 200%

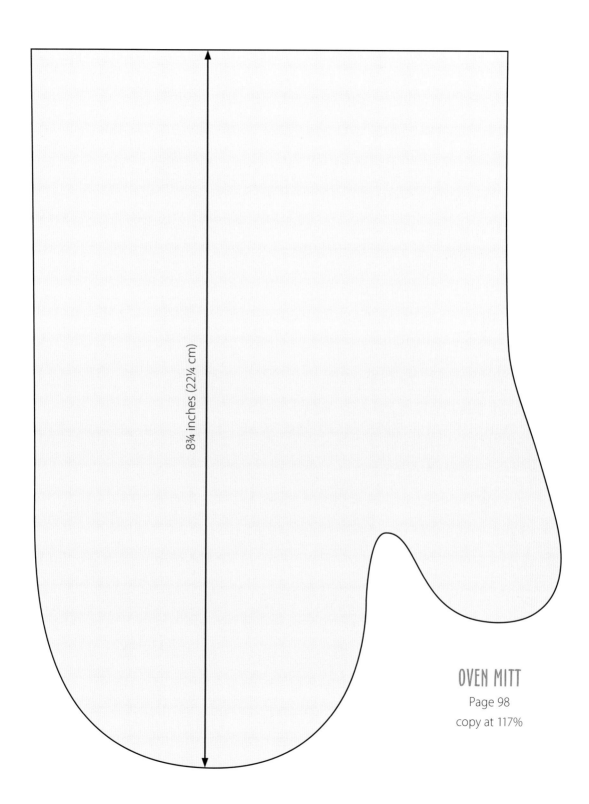

8¾ inches (22¼ cm)

OVEN MITT
Page 98
copy at 117%

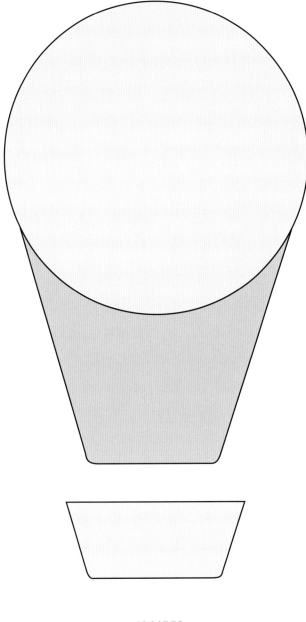

COASTER

Page 112

Actual Size

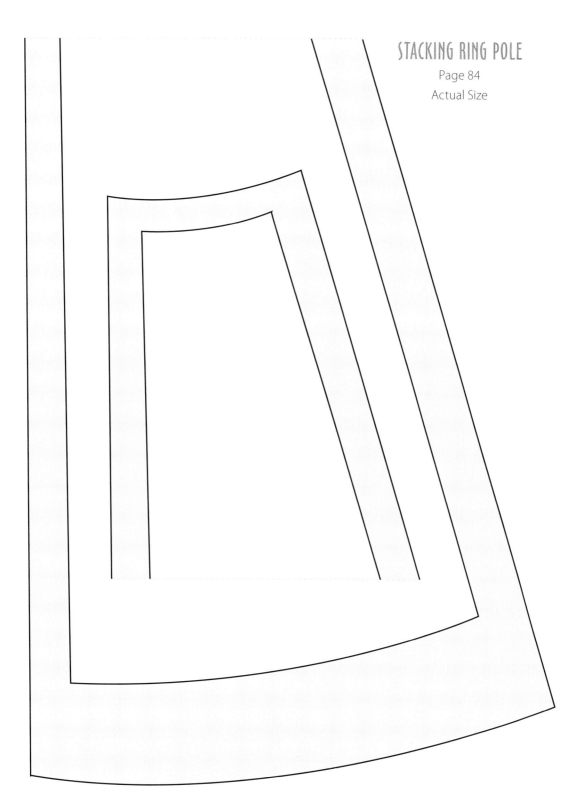

STACKING RING POLE
Page 84
Actual Size

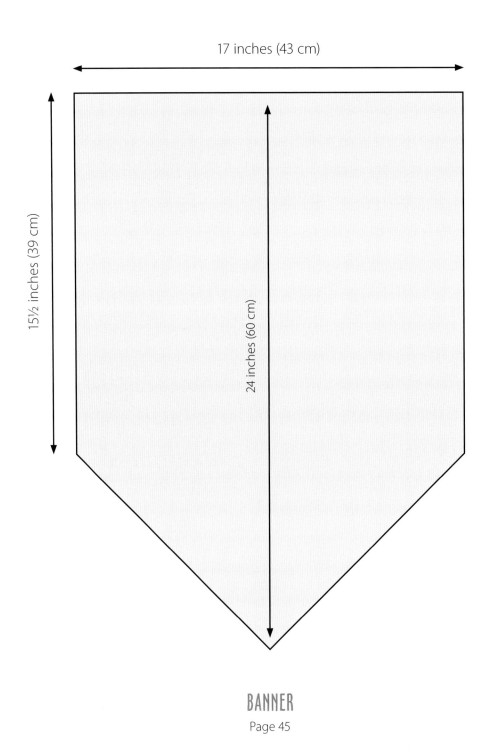

17 inches (43 cm)

15½ inches (39 cm)

24 inches (60 cm)

BANNER
Page 45

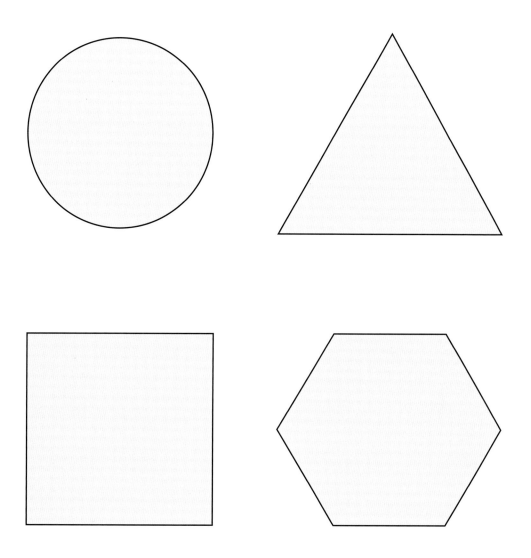

GEOMETRIC BUNTING
Page 74
Actual Size

INDEX

A
acetate, 213
acrylic, 213
appliqué, 38, 46, 182–183
aprons, 94, 100103

B
backpacks, 169, 172–175
banners, 26, 45–47, 171, 182–183, 220
basket liners, 123–124
beanbag chairs, 53, 61–62
bed runners, 56–58
bench cushions, 26, 42–44
binder covers, 55, 63–64, 178–179
bolster cushions, 26, 39–41
boxes, fabric-covered, 25, 28–30
bunting, geometric, 71, 74–75, 221

C
calico, 212
canvas backpacks, 169, 172–175
chair covers, 117, 128–129
cheesecloth, 212
cloud cushions, 59–60
coasters, 112–113, 218
coat hangers, 68–69
cord organizers, 147, 153–154
cotton, 213
covers
    boxes, 25, 28–30
    hot-water bottles, 49–51
    kitchen chairs, 117, 128–129
    notebooks, 55, 63–64
    stools, 71, 88–89
    tissue boxes, 25, 31–33
cushion pads, 213
cushions
    benches, 26, 42–44
    bolsters, 26, 39–41
    cloud-shaped, 59–60
    deck-chair headrest, 206–207
    garden cushions, 194–196
    jigsaw-shaped, 71, 82–83

D
deck chairs, 192, 205–207
denim organizers, 163–167
desk organizers, 169, 180–181
dish towels, 93, 108–109
door mufflers, 134, 135–136
doorstops, 134, 138
draft stoppers, 134, 139–141
duffel bags, 192, 202–204

E
embroidery hoops, 10–11

F
fabric boxes, 25, 28–30
fabric letters, 145, 151–152
fabric picture frames, 11, 22–23
fabric terminology, 212
fabric types, 213–214
fabrics, buying and using, 211
frayed napkins, 118

G
garden cushions, 194–196
gauze, 212
geometric bunting, 71, 74–75, 221

H
height chart, kite-shaped, 73, 76–78
hemstitch napkins, 118–122
hot-water-bottle covers, 49–51

I
ironing-board covers, 158–159
ironing-board organizer, 155–156

J
jean pockets, upcycling, 162–163, 167
jigsaw-shaped cushions, 71, 82–83

K
kimono, 54–55
kitchen chair covers, 117, 128–129
kite height chart, 73, 76–78

L

lampshades, 18
laundry bags, 10–11, 16–17
linen, 213

M

magazine files, 176–177
marking tools, 210
mitered corners, 121–122, 131
muslin, 212
muslin gauze, 212

N

napkins, 116, 118–122
natural fiber fabric, 213
needles, 210, 212
notebook covers, 55, 63–64, 178–179
nylon, 213

O

office organizers, 171, 184–185
organizers
    cord, 147, 153–154
    desk, 169, 180–181
    ironing-board, 155–156
    office, 171, 184–185
    wall, 163–167
oven mitts, 93, 98–99, 103, 217

P

picnic blankets, 193, 200–201
picture frames, 11, 22–23
pillowcases, 9, 12–13, 20–21
pinafores, 146–147, 160–161
pins, 210
place mats, 117, 125–126
plastic bag holders, 95, 104–105
play mats, 72–73, 79–81
pocket-front aprons, 94, 102–103
polyester, 213
pot holders, 93, 96–97

Q

quilting bed runners, 56–57
quilts, 215

R

rayon/viscose, 213
rotary cutters, 210

S

scissor cases, 187–189
scissors, 210
seam allowances, 211
seam rippers, 210
semi-synthetic fiber fabric, 214
sewing pinafores, 146–147, 160–161
sewing tools, 210
sewing-machine covers, 145, 148–150
silk, 213
slogan banner, 171, 182–183
spandex, 213
stacking rings, 84–87, 219
stool covers, 71, 88–89
storage trays, 65–67
The Stripes Company, 199
synthetic fiber fabric, 214

T

table runners, 130–131
tape measures, 210
tassels, 9, 14–15, 20–21
tea cozy, 95, 106–107, 216
thread, 210
tissue box covers, 25, 31–33
toilet-paper-roll holders, 27, 36–37
towels
    appliqué for, 38
    dish towels, 38, 93, 108–109
    patchwork, 27, 34–35
trays, 53, 65–67
trinket trays, 53

W

wall organizer, 163–167
weaving, 112–113
windbreak with pocket, 193, 197–199
wool, 213

Z

zigzag napkins, 118

ABOUT THE AUTHOR

Charlie Moorby is the editor of *Simply Sewing* magazine and has contributed to a number of *Mollie Makes* craft books. She writes two personal craft blogs: *The Savvy Crafter* (www.thesavvycrafter.co.uk) and *The Lucky Bluebird* (www.theluckybluebird.com).

Additional photographs provided by:
Project headers, needle and thread graphic: casejustin/Shutterstock
Pages 4 and 5, pins: Feng Yu/Shutterstock
Page 5, bottom right: Kostikova Natalia/Shutterstock
Page 16, bottom right, and page 152, bottom left: Seregam/Shutterstock
Page 17, bottom left: BW Folsom/Shutterstock
Page 18, bottom left, and page 207, bottom left: Africa Studio/Shutterstock
Page 23, bottom left: Hannamariah/Shutterstock
Page 31, bottom: Volodymyr Krasyuk/Shutterstock
Page 201, bottom left: Billion Photos/Shutterstock